# THE
# BRIDGE
# BUILDER'S
# STORY

## Also by Howard Fast

Seven Days in June

The Trial of Abigail Goodman

War and Peace (Essays)

Being Red: A Memoir

The Confession of Joe Cullen

The Pledge

The Dinner Party

Citizen Tom Paine (A Play)

The Immigrant's Daughter

The Outsider

Max

Time and the Riddle:
   Thirty-One Zen Stories

The Legacy

The Establishment

The Magic Door

Second Generation

The Immigrants

The Art of Zen Meditation

A Touch of Infinity

The Hessian

The Crossing

The General Zapped an Angel

The Jews: Story of a People

The Hunter and the Trap

Torquemada

The Hill

Agrippa's Daughter

Power

The Edge of Tomorrow

April Morning

The Golden River

The Winston Affair

Moses, Prince of Egypt

The Last Supper

Silas Timberman

The Passion of Sacco and Vanzetti

Spartacus

The Proud and the Free

Departure

My Glorious Brothers

Clarkton

The American

Freedom Road

Citizen Tom Paine

The Unvanquished

The Last Frontier

Conceived in Liberty

Place in the City

The Children

Strange Yesterday

Two Valleys

# THE BRIDGE BUILDER'S STORY

A Novel by

## HOWARD FAST

*M.E. Sharpe*

Armonk, New York • London, England

**Library of Congress Cataloging-in Publication Data**

Fast, Howard, 1914–
The bridge builder's story : a novel / Howard Fast.
p.    cm.
ISBN 1-56324-691-0 (alk. paper)
I. Title.
PS3511.A784B75    1995
813′.52—dc20
95-11018
CIP


Printed in the United States of America


The paper used in this publication meets the minimum requirements of
American National Standard for Information Sciences—
Permanence of Paper for Printed Library Materials,
ANSI Z 39.48-1984.


∞


MV (c)    10    9    8    7    6    5    4    3    2    1

*To Bette Fast*

wife, companion and lover
for fifty-seven years

# THE
# BRIDGE
# BUILDER'S
# STORY

# Part One

# Berlin

# I

My name is Scott Waring. On the sixth of May, 1939, I was married to Martha Pembroke. The wedding took place at ten o'clock in the morning, and at four o'clock on that same afternoon, we sailed to Europe on the *Queen Mary*. We left the ship at Cherbourg and took the boat train to Paris.

I put this down as a beginning. The beginning of a person's story is a matter of choice. You can start at birth, or even before birth; but when I think about it, I suppose my story really began when my grandfather gave me an automatic pistol on my sixteenth birthday.

I always felt that my grandfather—of whom I was quite fond—was a foolish old man, a colonel in World War One, with all sorts of notions that I rejected entirely; nevertheless, I accepted his gift, to my father's displeasure.

The pistol was a Webley 30-calibre automatic, a beautifully machined gun, one of only two hundred manufactured, a line so high-priced that it was soon discontinued. I suppose

I felt some kind of spurious manliness in possessing it. I never fired the gun.

When I married Martha, I had finished my junior year as an engineering student at the Massachusetts Institute of Technology. Martha had completed her second year at Wellesley College. We met the year before at an inter-college dance and fell madly in love. People held that we were well-suited to each other, and indeed we had come from similar backgrounds, upper middle class, well-to-do even during the depression years. Martha was one of two sisters; I myself have a sister a few years older. We had both been coddled, cared for, and loved; our lives were quite sheltered—that is, until our honeymoon trip to Europe. Martha was a tall, good-looking woman, blue-eyed, with naturally blond hair. My mother liked her, defining her as a "sensible" person, very high praise from my mother. As for myself, I am six feet in height, have brown hair and greenish eyes, and am a middling to fair athlete.

The crossing on the *Queen Mary* was quite wonderful. Handsome, well-to-do and personable young people have doors opened to them easily. We were seated at the captain's table. At the evening dances, I had to struggle for a place on Martha's ticket, against a covey of handsome young British officers. That was a time when first-class passage on the *Queen* put an ultimate definition on luxury.

Beside Martha and myself and the captain, five others shared the big round table. There was a British couple, Sir

Arthur Creel, and his wife, Lady Jane Creel, Franklin Holden, an American businessman, one of our largest plastic manufacturers, his wife, Libby, and finally, Wolf Horstmann, German consul-general in New York, on his way to join his wife in Paris for a holiday. I specify each of them because, having brooded over this, I feel that Horstmann's presence and the conversations around that dinner table had a good deal to do with events that followed.

I must say that the captain's table was an unusual treat for Martha and me. The captain, Ian MacGregor, was a delightful host. I learned that he always chose his table companions carefully. In this case, Holden had intentions of merging his business with a British plastics manufacturer, and Creel was an important figure in British politics. Horstmann, a handsome, personable man, was a diplomat of considerable importance, and I suppose that Martha and I were included both as window dressing and because my father had recently joined President Roosevelt's staff as a special military advisor. All in all, the captain's table seated a worldly and sophisticated group, that is, excepting Martha and myself.

There was one evening of conversation, the third night out, that I recall very well. By then, as happens on a trans-Atlantic crossing—that was before air travel took over—reticence had broken down. First-class passengers were upper-class passengers, and in the world of dinner jackets and manners, a tribal intimacy prevailed. Holden and Creel had exchanged some thoughts about the possibility that England would not be drawn into a European conflict, and Horstmann expressed a belief that there would be no European war.

"War," he said, "oh, certainly the very last thing in the world that Germany needs." His English was excellent, with only a trace of accent. "You must understand that we lived through hard and bitter years after 1918, and suffering and hunger make for long memories. These six years under Chancellor Hitler have changed that. The German people have learned what it is to have a pot of meat on the table, a loaf of bread. They work and they are well paid. They have good homes to live in—but war? My goodness, war destroys everything. We don't want war."

"I do wish you could convince us of that," Lady Creel said.

"Unfortunately," Horstmann said, "your press writes otherwise. This is something we can't compete with."

"Perhaps the people who write for our newspapers think about Austria and Czechoslovakia," Martha said. She had a childlike quality of innocence about her, which impelled some people to decide that her brain was as innocent as her smile. Actually, she had a better handle on what was happening to the world than I did. Political Science was her major in college.

To my surprise, Horstmann nodded respectfully. "Absolutely, my dear. But when maps are drawn by a conqueror, the conquered have little to say about it. Both Austria and the Sudeten are German lands. Your press gives little credence to this."

"Oh, really, sir!" Libby Holden burst out. She was a fussily dressed lady in her mid forties, a former associate editor of the *Ladies' Home Journal.* "And if the fact that Austrians speak German entitles you to call them Germans, then I would ask Sir Arthur here to give up his citizenship and become an American."

Horstmann clapped his hands and said, "Touché, dear lady!"

"On the other hand," Lady Jane pointed out, "perhaps our American cousins should change places. We had the language before your Pilgrim fathers ever set foot on Plymouth Rock."

"Will no one say a word in my defense?" Horstmann asked, smiling to show that he was not at all troubled by criticism.

"Come now, Mr. Waring," Captain MacGregor said, turning the conversation away from Horstmann, "you have the ear of Mr. Roosevelt. What is his opinion of war or no war?"

"I hardly have the ear of the President," I said. "Actually, I've never met him."

"Forgive my curiosity," Holden said, "but what makes the captain think that you might have the ear of the President?"

Martha looked at me strangely—a warning glance, possibly. I don't know. I try to piece together what happened aboard ship, but it was a long time ago. Anyway, I saw no reason to be silent about such things.

"My father has been working at the White House these past few months."

"Of course," Libby Holden said. "I should have made the connection. Your father is Charles Waring. It was in the papers," she explained to the others.

Obviously embarrassed, Sir Arthur said, "I really don't think it's any of our affair."

"A cabinet appointment?" Holden wondered. "I don't recall any."

"No, he's there as a consultant."

"You see," Horstmann explained, "Mr. Waring, like any son of a famous father, is reluctant to speak of him. I understand that. Perhaps my presence inhibits him. It should not. The war was a long time ago."

"Why on earth should your presence inhibit him?" Libby Holden wondered.

Horstmann looked at me questioningly.

"My father is his own person," I said. "We're very close. And anyway, it's public knowledge. As far as his being a consultant to the President, well, that is something we've never discussed."

"Of course," Horstmann agreed.

"I would love to be enlightened," Lady Jane said. "Dear Mr. Waring, the bitter truth is that people love nothing more than gossip. So please tell me the terrible truth about your father—unless it's too terrible. Then, of course, you must only whisper it."

"Jane!" her husband snorted.

I looked at Martha hopelessly, and she said, "The terrible

truth, Lady Jane, is that Scott's father is an airplane manufacturer—"

"A very small one," I put in.

"But a very good one, and some months ago, the *New York
Herald Tribune* ran a story about a new warplane that Scott's
father had designed."

"Hardly very terrible," Lady Jane observed. "I'm disap-
pointed."

"You're impossible," her husband said.

Unwilling to let go of it, Libby Holden insisted on knowing why Horstmann's presence should have inhibited me.

"Because, my dear lady," Horstmann said, "this young
man's father, Charles Waring, was one of the great aces during the unhappy war of 1914. He shot down twenty-three
German planes. But that was a long time ago, and I can only
admire his daring and courage. The only part of that
wretched war that was admirable was the single man-to-man
combat between aviators. Wouldn't you agree with me, Mr.
Waring?"

I shrugged. I had no intentions of getting into an ideologi-
cal discussion with Wolf Horstmann, and I had no intention
of disrupting the pleasure of dining at the captain's table. At
the moment, the coffee came, and with it our desserts. The
food, I must mention, was wonderful, every dish a small triumph, putting to rest the current legend of the deplorable
quality of British food. After dinner, we left the ladies briefly
and went into the lounge to smoke our cigars, a habit I had

inherited, along with the Webley automatic, as a birthday gift from my grandfather. He had waited until I was a student at MIT before presenting me with my first box of cigars, remarking that it would at least keep me away from cigarettes.

Horstmann, seated in an easy chair alongside me, presented me with one of his cigars, an expensive Cuban panatela. I was leaning over backwards at this point to be pleasant. For the first two nights, I had admired his silky and cosmopolitan ease; tonight, my admiration turned to distaste—yet I mistrusted my own feelings. I was young, and his very sophisticated approach made me hesitate to group him with the black-shirted thugs who were serving Adolf Hitler and bringing the new German order into being.

Now, in the smoking lounge, he was thoughtful, flattering me with his interest in my future. He asked questions about MIT, and what branch of engineering I had selected. I felt boyish and a bit foolish as I told him of my dreams of building great bridges, as, for example, the new and amazing George Washington Bridge in New York.

"Yet I would have thought," he said, "that a military career would be more to your choosing. After all, considering your family background, it would appear logical."

"My family background?" I wondered what and why he knew anything about my background—anything more than my father's reputation.

As if he read my thoughts, he replied, "A part of being a

consul-general in New York. One learns about the important families."

"Mine is hardly an important family." I was letting myself become irritated.

"Your grandfather was General Pershing's aide. Modesty is commendable. I was not trying to pry."

"Of course," I said shortly. A long moment of silence. There were three more days of dining together, and I tried to be more friendly. "I don't think we have such a thing as a military family—that is, in the European sense. My father loves flying, but the first time I went up with him, I was scared to death. I'm a sort of half-baked pacifist, if that makes any sense. My father never tried to change my thinking."

"Very sensible of him."

Later that evening, I walked on the deck with Martha, and I told her of my conversation with Horstmann. "At first," she said, "I was fascinated with him. He makes a romantic figure with that thatch of blond hair and his bit of a German accent. Now he frightens me a little. Why should he know about your family?"

"Gramps was involved in the armaments business. Not so much as he likes to make out, but he ran errands for Pershing and he rates a footnote in the history books."

"Scott, why don't you like him?"

"Horstmann?"

"I mean your grandfather. He's a nice old man, and he was a darling to me."

"He's a darling to any pretty woman of any age, and he refuses to face the fact that he's past seventy—hell, no. That has nothing to do with it. He's a war lover."

"And he says that sooner or later we'll be at war. Have you thought about that?"

"I've thought about it."

"Anyway," Martha said, "I'm glad we're going to Europe while it's still there."

Later in our walk on the deck, Sir Arthur and his wife joined us. Martha and Lady Jane fell back a few steps, and I could hear her instructing Martha on the virtues of Paris shops. Sir Arthur spoke quietly: "I saw you talking to Horstmann."

"Oh? Yes. He appears to be interested in my family."

"It's probably none of my business, Scott, but I would be careful of what I might say to him."

"Really? Aside from the German thing, he seems to be decent enough. Usually, he's quite charming. I don't know why I was put off by him tonight."

"It's not just that he's a German. He's a Nazi, and a damned important Nazi. That's why he's posted to New York. I'm sure you know why Roosevelt drafted your father into Washington?"

I was not sure I did know. "Well, this new fighter plane of his—I mean it would take a pile of cash to put it into production, and the government would have to be involved in that. But that would be air force procurement, wouldn't it?"

"More than that, from what I hear, Scott. Your country needs an air force, and they don't have one to speak of. Neither do we—certainly not in terms of the game Adolf Hitler plays. The likely thing is that your dad is there to help build it, and that would be of immense interest to Wolf Horstmann."

# II

On our fifth day in Paris, Martha said, "A wise God—a woman, mind you, because my God is a woman—who decided to grant a paradise to our poor souls, could not do better than Paris."

"Absolutely. For Americans. The French are already here."

We were not only doing Paris, we were drunk with it. Oh, we wore ourselves out in the Louvre, but that was duty and no place for lovers. Places like the Tuileries Gardens allowed us to create our own world of fantasy. The sidewalk cafes were cloaked in jewels of our delight, and we communed with the people who saw us and smiled with pleasure. We were egotistical and uncaring, and we were beautiful to look at and beautiful to each other. We made love each night with the certainty that we had invented the practice and that no one else had ever made love as we did. Hand in hand, we walked through the wonderful old streets that were home to Cézanne and Renoir and Hugo and Zola and Aragon, and we paraded our store of knowledge before each other, and we were equally delighted at how remarkable we were.

We never paused to entertain the notion that we were a bit foolish. I was twenty-one years old; Martha was nineteen.

On a high hill, the city dancing in the sunlight beneath us, Martha proposed a future. In the month of May in Paris, all dreams are possible. She laid it out simply and directly. A year from now, when I finished with the Massachusetts Institute of Technology, we would take off for France. She would dump her last year at Wellesley, and instead of my burrowing away in some "dusty old engineering job," as she put it, we'd spend a year in Paris.

"Doing what?" I asked her.

"Being in Paris," she said blithely. "It's not a matter of doing. Being here with each other is all the doing we need."

"And what do we live on?"

"We have six thousand dollars in wedding cash. We can stretch that out for two years. Everything is ridiculously cheap here."

"A reasonable future," I agreed. We were lunching at a cafe, with a bottle of red table wine and a basket full of the best bread in the world, and two omelets like mountains of glistening gold. I decided that the two-year advantage I had over Martha entitled me to be just a bit more practical, and I reminded her that spring in Paris gave way to summer, and summer to winter, and in winter reality had a habit of returning.

"Then let's stay here. Right here. Right now."

"We have tickets and hotel reservations for Berlin and for Vienna and for Budapest."

"Let's skip them all," Martha said. "The more I read about Germany, the less I want to go there."

"My dear lovely Martha," I told her gravely, "I have been studying this wretched German language for seven years, because my father said that an engineer must have German, and as much as I wish I had never listened to him, I must use it some time. Wolf Horstmann said my German was excellent, and that with a bit of practice, I could pass as a Prussian—"

"And that's what you want—to pass as a Prussian?"

"No. No, of course not. But it all fascinates me."

"Why?"

"I suppose because it's so bizarre, so unbelievable—I mean here in the twentieth century for that crazy society to come into being. I want to see it."

"That's morbid."

"No, my dear, no—well, maybe, maybe a little. Your French is wonderful, but I sit by and listen to you babble away to everyone we meet, and I can't even order a meal properly—"

She shook her head hopelessly.

"Well," I said, "if you feel so strongly about it—"

"No. Oh, no. We shouldn't begin that way, and you're right. It will be an adventure, won't it?"

Yet it was less of an adventure, at least at the beginning, than we had imagined. Our suite at the Adlon Hotel on unter den Linden was splendid beyond belief. Martha shrugged and asked what did I expect from a travel agent who had been told to charge it all to my father? Climbing into the huge bed, with its purple and gold coverlet, was like diving into a morass of feathers and silk, and Martha remarked that for the first time she understood the divide between opulence and taste. The bedroom walls were covered with silk rather than wallpaper, the silk slightly threadbare, and the furniture in the sitting room was upholstered in gold-threaded satin. "Nothing touched since the days of the Kaiser," I told her.

"But clean, you must admit that."

"Disgustingly clean."

In the morning, we ordered breakfast in our room. Two young women appeared, wheeling into the sitting room, through the double doors, a large table, set for two, with coffee, eggs, ham and sausage, fruit, hard bread, sweet bread, cakes and whipped cream.

"I don't believe it," Martha said. "According to the newspapers, they were all starving."

"I'll bet there are few breakfasts like this outside of the Adlon. Everything for the tourists. The blessings of the Fuhrer."

"What do we do with it?"

"Eat, drink and be merry."

"Scott, I don't think I'll be merry until we get out of Berlin. The place is spooky. Everyone acts as if nothing has happened, no *Kristallnacht*—is that what they call it?—when they smashed all the Jewish shops, no invasion of Austria, no invasion of Czechoslovakia, no Gestapo, just happy people in a happy city. No, I am not going to eat this ridiculous breakfast."

I poured coffee. "Rolls, butter, the stewed fruit is excellent, prunes, apricots—"

"I hate prunes. I've always hated prunes."

"There you are. I thought I knew everything about you. You ate stewed fruit in Paris."

"In Paris it tasted good."

"You haven't tasted this."

"In Paris everything tasted good."

I poured another cup of coffee, buttered a roll, which I gingerly passed on to Martha, and then I opened a guide book. "It says here—now listen carefully, young lady, it says here, 'Berlin is perhaps the most dynamic of all European cities. Its broad boulevards and splendid public buildings and palaces are unmatched, even in Paris. Its parks are unique, veritable gardens of trees. And the whole city sparkles with a type of cleanliness unmatched anywhere—' "

"The angels sing. Berlin is clean."

"Sarcasm from the sweetest lass in Wellesley. I never suspected it. Well, we live and we learn. A marriage made in heaven comes unglued in Berlin."

"Scott Waring, don't tell me you like this place?"

I sang to her, "I wish that I were back again, in the tech on Boylston Street, dressed in my dinky uniform, so dapper and so neat—"

"Scott!"

19

"Do you remember my room there, eight by twelve? And you said it was darling. This room—well."

"We could check out tomorrow and go to Vienna."

I went to her and kissed her. "We have only three days here, and the weather is lovely, so we can walk around and look at things, and when we come home, everyone will say, you really went to Berlin and you saw that horror with your own eyes. You know, if you read German, honey, Hegel, Schelling, Goethe—you know, there was an architect, name of Schinkel, and they say he set the style for all of the great buildings in Europe, and his work is all over Berlin, and we'll hire one of those strange old carriages they have in front of the hotel, and we'll ride all over the place, and you'll be amazed at my spectacular German."

"You're a very sweet man," she said to me. "I'm glad I married you. I never told you about the dreadful argument I had with my father. It wasn't that he didn't approve of you, but he felt that I was too young to know my own mind— that's the way he put it—and he insisted that I finish college. Well, anyway, I have the most wonderful linen suit, made for riding in a carriage."

So it was and so it happened, and that first full day in Berlin was glorious. Back at the hotel, we heard that the following afternoon, Adolf Hitler would speak—an unscheduled public address from the steps of the Reichstag, which was at the eastern border of the Tiergarten, within sight of the Brandenburg Gate. I felt that to be able to hear Adolf

Hitler give one of his hypnotic, ranting speeches, so many of which we had seen on the Pathé News screen, was an historic event not to be missed. Martha thought it might well be missed, but gave in to my wishes. It was my doing, my wish, my stupidity.

Long afterwards, I was asked, "Were you followed? Was your room bugged?" Followed? Bugged? We wouldn't have dreamed of such a thing. I go into some detail about our backgrounds in an attempt to explain what sort of kids we were. We had babbled of all our plans in the presence of Wolf Horstmann, our intentions of going to Berlin, to Vienna and to Budapest, our feeling of disgust about Adolf Hitler and what had happened in Germany. I had spoken of a Jewish professor at MIT, with whom I had taken a class in physics, who was perhaps the most brilliant and innovative man I had ever encountered. Martha's great-grandfather was Jewish, and he had been a secretary of commerce or some such thing in the Confederate government during the Civil War, and she had held forth, at the captain's table, about a government that would have damned her for that connection.

With that was the sense—a quality of youth and love—that we were immortal and indestructible, and a cloak of innocence and pleasure enhanced that feeling.

So we went to the rally at the Reichstag and became a part of the gathering crowd. The front of the Reichstag building, repaired after the fire of six years before, was draped with enormous swastika-blazoned flags. A wooden stage had been

built, and in front of it were two ranks of black-shirted SS
men. To one side were six trumpeters, each with a long silver
trumpet, and the stand itself was surrounded with swastika
banners. At the other side of the stand there was a seating
area that was filling up with a mixture of men in civilian
clothes and men in bemedaled uniforms. We had come early,
and we were able to find a place well toward the speaker's
platform. I listened to the talk of the people around me,
translating bits of this and that for Martha. We were obviously tourists, dressed differently—the natives wore dark
business suits, the women drab dresses—and bystanders plied
us with questions. I chattered away in German. Yes, we were
Americans. And what did we think of the Fuhrer's Germany?
Very nice, very clean. I translated for Martha, who giggled.
And do you see how he, our Fuhrer, is loved? You have such
strange notions about Germany in America.

They were delighted with a tourist who could speak German so fluently, and they helped us forward, so that we
might get a better look at the *wunderbar* Adolf. By now, the
crowd had increased to a size that took it back into the
Tiergarten, and there was a great fanfare from the trumpets,
and Adolf Hitler emerged from the Reichstag and took his
place at the speaker's stand.

Now the thought occurred to me. Mind you, it was a
thought, only a thought. I had never fired a gun, I had never
wanted to fire a gun; and if I were to fire a pistol, I would not
be able to hit the side of a barn. But the thought was heady

and delicious. There I was, no more than forty or fifty yards from where Adolf Hitler was shouting at the crowd to recognize and accept their manifest destiny, and in the side pocket of my jacket was the Webley automatic pistol that my grandfather had given me. In Paris, it had reposed safely in a suitcase. But here in Berlin, where I had sold myself a stupid set of possibilities and dangers, I had decided to carry it; and now, simply as an accompaniment to my fantasy, I put my hand into the side pocket of my jacket and closed it over the butt of the Webley.

And at that moment, a man materialized on my right side and gripped my wrist—with the kind of grip that feels like an iron vise. Another man, tall, brawny, hard-faced, gripped my left arm, and I felt the hard nose of a gun jammed into my body under my ribs. When the man on the right grabbed my wrist, I let go of the Webley. The man on my left said softly, in German, "One move, you bastard, and I'll rip your guts open." The man on my right reached into my pocket, took out the Webley, and dropped it into his own pocket. Two more men were moving Martha through the crowd, a bewildered, frightened Martha, vainly struggling to get free. I tried struggling, and the gun pressed tighter into my side.

I was half-dragged after Martha, yelling at them to leave her alone; and she twisted around to look at me, pleading, "Scott, tell them—tell them who we are! Scott, for God's sake, tell them that we're American citizens! Scott, why?"

"Leave her alone, damn you!" I shouted.

It was a small, feeble effort. This was my first encounter with violence, and I don't know whether I was more frightened than enraged, indeed outraged that two American citizens should be put upon in this fashion; and there was Martha, separated from me and dragged away like a piece of luggage.

The crowd gave way before us, as if they had been rehearsed. There were no expressions of anger, no expressions of sympathy, no expressions at all, just blank faces turned away; and we were quickly moved through the crowd. Still vainly struggling and protesting, we were moved, dragged, walked, to a place where cars were parked. Martha was pushed into one car. I was pushed into another, and we were driven away. As we were separated, Martha cried out, "Scott, help me!" For the moment, I lost all fear and struggled like a madman to free myself and reach her. One of the men who held me hit me hard across the face with the back of his hand, blurring my sight. My eyes filled with tears of pain and rage, and through my blurred vision I saw the car door close behind Martha.

In the car, I was seated between the two men who had dragged me through the crowd, and we drove to what I later learned was Prinz-Albrecht-Gelände, the site of Gestapo headquarters. I was then taken out of the car and into the Gestapo building. I looked around for the car that held Martha, but there was no sign of it. They took me into the building, into the main foyer, a broad, high-ceilinged room, decorated with swastika banners and bronze eagles.

"Where is my wife?" I demanded, speaking German. "This

is insane! You have no right to arrest us! We've done nothing!"

They ignored me. The man who had taken the gun from me said to a man in uniform who sat at an ornate desk, "Scott Waring."

The man in uniform picked up the phone that sat on his desk, punched the cradle, and spoke into the phone: "Schwartz—with the American, Waring." He listened for a moment, and then said to the man named Schwartz, "Room eleven."

# III

oom eleven was eighteen or twenty feet square. It had no windows, and the walls were painted a sort of hospital green. On one wall, there was what appeared to be a frame, say five by eight, but the frame contained nothing. Next to the frame, there were several light switches. The room was lit by a set of incandescent tubes on the ceiling. There was a table, plain, unfinished wood, with an enameled metal top, much like a large kitchen table. There were six chairs in the room. I would have called them kitchen chairs.

The same two men who had taken me out of the crowd escorted me up a broad flight of stairs and down a corridor to room eleven. They opened the door, pushed me inside, closed the door behind me and left me there. I tried the door immediately. It was deadlocked. Then I prowled around the bleak, empty room, trying to get my wits together and to get a hold on myself. When I held out my hand as a measure of my condition, it was still shaking.

I sat down and worked at some reassuring thoughts. Neither Martha nor I, surely, were run-of-the-mill tourists. We came from reasonably important families. Her father was the editor of a national magazine. My father was working with the government. They had arranged to telephone us at the Adlon before we left for Vienna. They would call. Inquiries would be made at the Embassy. However unpleasant our present condition was, certainly it would be over soon. As soon as we came before a judge or a justice of the peace— surely they had the equivalent of these—we could tell our side of the story and we would be released. Germany might be an unpleasant country, but it was a civilized country, a part of Europe and a country that had diplomatic relations with the United States. The thing for me to do was to get hold of myself, overcome my fear, and be ready to state our case; and as I calmed down, my heart went out to Martha—to my dearest, my most innocent Martha.

They had not taken my wristwatch, so I can say that I sat alone for a full half hour—which felt like an eternity. Then the door opened, and two men in civilian clothes entered. They were very ordinary-looking men, one small and stout with glasses, the other large and heavy. The small man introduced himself and the other, speaking heavily accented English: "Mr. Kreutzer, here, and me, Mr. Roldtmann. Shall we speak English, yes, Mr. Waring?"

My German was certainly better than his English. "German," I said, "and I demand to know the meaning of this. My wife and I are on our honeymoon. We are American citizens. How dare you arrest us and brutally drag us here? We have done nothing. I demand the right to speak to our Embassy— and I want to see my wife."

"Your German is excellent," Kreutzer agreed. The manner of both men was amiable, and I began to feel better.

"On the other hand," Roldtmann said, "your arrest is not without reason. You had an automatic pistol in your pocket; you were within shot of our Chancellor; and when we intervened, I am told, your hand was on the butt of your pistol and you were ready to draw it. So you can hardly claim that your arrest was without reason."

"I had no intention of using the pistol."

"So you say, so you say."

"I want to see my wife."

"All in good time. You will see your wife. She has come to no harm. Meanwhile, we must talk and clear up certain matters. Now, please sit down here and make yourself comfortable." He indicated the table. I took a chair at one side. The two men seated themselves opposite me. They were both so matter-of-fact that I began to take heart and arrange some explanations in my mind.

"About the gun—" I began.

"Please! We will talk about the gun later." That was Kreutzer. He took a small black notebook from his pocket and opened it on the table. "First, we talk about yourself. To begin with, you say that you and your wife are simply tourists on your honeymoon. Be that as it may, why Berlin? You are neither friend nor admirer of the Third Reich or our Chancellor."

"Berlin is a beautiful city. I have studied German for years. That is why I wanted to see both Berlin and Vienna. Is that so strange?"

"Perhaps not," Kreutzer agreed. "No single piece of a jig-saw puzzle is meaningful in itself. But suppose we look closer at the whole picture. We'll begin with your grandfather, Daniel Brookfield Waring. Three months ago, he was re-commissioned as a full colonel in the United States Army, attached to Army Intelligence."

"Ah, no—my grandfather!" It was news to me. "He's an old windbag."

"Evidently your General Staff does not think so. The unit to which he has been attached specializes in counter-intelligence, which is a grab-bag containing, among other things, assassination."

"Ridiculous! Our army does not go in for assassination!"

"Your father," Kreutzer continued, "was a famous ace in the last war. He was recently called down to Washington, where he has the ear of your President Roosevelt. He has recently developed a new kind of warplane. There is much about your father, Charles Waring, that we know; there is much that we don't know; and there are numerous facts that we surmise, but not without reason. As far as your wife is concerned, she is hardly the innocent you propose her to be.

In her second year in college, she wrote a term paper on Mata Hari, who as you may or may not know, was a woman named Margaretha Zelle, a famous spy in the service of our high command during the past war."

I simply could not believe what I was hearing. That this romantic essay by Martha should be given a sinister purpose was incredible—indeed the whole ridiculous patchwork quilt was incredible. Where did they get their information, I asked myself? How on God's earth could they have found a student's term paper at Wellesley College? If United States Army Intelligence was foolish enough to appoint a silly old man like my grandfather to an important post, it meant only that Army Intelligence hardly lived up to its name.

Kreutzer then took some sheets of paper from his jacket pocket and unfolded them on the table, smoothing the creases carefully. "Let me read this to you. You will forgive my accent, but I read this in English because it was recorded in English. It is a conversation with your wife in your suite at the Adlon." Then he read:

> MARTHA: Are you going to take that dumb gun with you?
>
> SCOTT: Why not? In this demented land, it might even come in handy.
>
> MARTHA: Handy for what?
>
> SCOTT: Who knows! If I get close enough to the monster, I might just pop him. That would change history, wouldn't it?
>
> MARTHA: I love it when you do the gangster, Scott. You're so unsuited to it. I bet you couldn't hit the side of a barn.

SCOTT: Trouble is, women have this notion that they know everything about the men they marry. For all you know, I might be the number one crackerjack marksman in the whole U.S.A. After all, I do come from a family of military clowns.

Kreutzer finished reading, looked up and stared at me—and I felt sick. How do you explain crazy talk? How do you explain the silly things lovers say to one another? How do you explain hyperbole to people who have not a shred of humor?

"We were joking. We were playing games."

"Can you explain the joke?" Kreutzer asked softly. "That's what we are here for. To understand."

"There's nothing to understand. Why don't you examine the pistol? It has never been fired. I never fired a gun in my life. I hate guns. All right—we don't love your Fuhrer, but is that a crime? You hate President Roosevelt, and even if you shouted it on Broadway and Forty-second Street, no one would arrest you!"

"That's all you have to say, Mr. Waring?"

"What else can I say? These are innocent things—all right, stupid actions, childish, but innocent."

"We don't think so."

"Then what do you think? What can you think? Do you imagine that we are involved in some crazy scheme to kill Hitler?"

Roldtmann, who had said very little, now smiled, the first

smile of the day. "Yes, that is exactly what we think. We think that you are neck deep in something very large and very important, and Herr Kreutzer, here, and myself, it is our duty to protect the Fuhrer, and we intend to do our duty."

"All right," I said, "that's enough. I demand the right to call the American Embassy."

"No," Kreutzer said.

The fear was back now, and with it all the horrible stories I had read about the Gestapo, the torture chambers, the secret murders, the way people disappeared, never to be heard of again.

"I want to see my wife."

"Of course. But you have a great deal to tell us."

"I have nothing to tell you. What will you do to me—beat me, whip me, pull out my fingernails? You know, this whole thing is absolutely insane."

"We are not going to beat you," Kreutzer said. "We are not going to pull out your fingernails. And we will allow you to see your wife. Turn your chair around."

For a moment, I didn't understand what he meant.

"Turn your chair around and face that wall," he said, pointing to the wall with the framed area and the row of switches. I now noticed a small area, perhaps six inches by six inches, outside the frame and covered by some sort of mesh. Kreutzer flicked a switch and spoke into this mesh: "I'm switching in now."

He flicked another switch, and the framed-in area lit up. It was a one-way mirror, plainly revealing a room almost identical to the room we were in. Martha sat in a chair, and two burly men, each stripped to the waist, stood facing her. Her eyes were red and there were tears on her cheeks.

"There is your wife," Kreutzer said. "Obviously, she has not been harmed," he continued in a conversational tone, "and whether she will be harmed is up to you."

"Let me talk to her, please."

"I'm afraid not."

"Can she see us?"

"No."

"Well, what do you mean, it's up to me? How is it up to me? I'll do anything, but don't harm her."

"We take no pleasure in such things, whatever you have been told. But unless you are willing to throw some light on your mission here, she will be increasingly uncomfortable."

"I don't know what I can tell you. For God's sake, believe me, please!"

"Do you want to think about it for a few minutes?"

"I told you the truth."

Kreutzer shook his head and stared at me unhappily. "Put yourself in my place, Mr. Waring. I serve the Fuhrer. I am sworn to protect him. I have no alternative."

"I am begging you. Do whatever you have to do to me. But leave her alone."

"Those men are stripped to the waist, not to reveal their physiques, but to keep their clothes from becoming bloody. If that sounds threatening, I must agree that it is."

Kreutzer nodded at Roldtmann, and Roldtmann went to the panel of switches, pressed one, and said, "Begin."

I shouted, "No, no, no!"

One of the bare-chested men in the next room reached down to Martha, grabbed her dress at the throat, and tore it away. I saw her lips move as she cried out, but heard no sound. Then, with the back of his hand, he struck her across the face, knocking her out of the chair onto the floor. As she lay there, knees drawn up, the other man clutched her under her arms and flung her back into the chair, where she sat crouched, arms crossed to cover her naked breasts. As the man lifted his clenched fist to strike her, I cried out, "Enough! Enough—I'll tell you everything! Everything!"

Roldtmann pressed the switch. "Stop!" he said.

Too late. The blow struck her face, knocking her out of the chair again, and she lay on the floor, blood running from her nose. I went crazy, leaping at Roldtmann, yelling, "You killed her, you bastard! You killed her!"

Kreutzer grabbed me from behind, pinning my arms, while I screamed curses at Roldtmann. Roldtmann pressed the switch and said, "Schwartz, get a nurse and both of you get out of there." The violence washed out of me. I was no good at violence, I knew nothing about it. Kreutzer let go of me. I pressed up against the glass. Martha stirred, and I saw her lips move. Thank God she's alive, I was telling myself. The two naked-to-the-waist brutes had left the room. Now a woman in a nurse's uniform and a man in a white coat entered. They bent over Martha, and Roldtmann snapped a switch and the mirror went dark.

"They will take care of her," Kreutzer said. "She is not badly hurt. I am glad you came to your senses. I do not enjoy such things, and I hope we shall not have to resume our punishment." He led me back to my chair.

"I want to see her," I said.

"All in due time. Be content with the fact that you have saved her pain and misery. First, we talk, and you tell us the whole story. That is the price you pay to save her life."

"Not until I see her and speak to her."

Kreutzer sighed. "That is impossible. You will either tell us what you agreed to tell us, or her punishment will resume."

My head was spinning. I had just watched Martha being savagely beaten. A few minutes more of such beating would kill her. I have gone over that time a thousand times. I was thinking desperately, using a mind that was coming apart, and there is no way to describe my agony at that moment. I had no doubts about what Kreutzer said would happen. Twenty-four hours ago, I could not have believed that a scene like this was possible, that two men would beat a woman to death, and that two other men would watch complacently while the execution took place. For the moment, I appeared to have saved her life by agreeing to reveal the details of a plot that did not exist. I realized that I was crying, and I reached for a handkerchief to wipe my eyes. Kreutzer took a small flask out of his jacket pocket. "Brandy. Drink some. You'll feel better."

I took a swallow, coughed, choked. I tried to pull myself together. Roldtmann left the room.

"What will happen to my wife if I tell you everything?" I asked him, trying hopelessly to put together something that I might tell them that would not sound totally insane. But would anything sound insane in a land as insane as this and in a situation as insane as this?

"Your wife will be all right."

"How do I know? Why should I believe you?"

"Because I say so." He shrugged. "You have seen the situation, Mr. Waring. What is, is. It's as simple as that. You have no recourse. If the information is complete, valuable, and can be confirmed, there will be reason for us to be grateful."

And do what, I asked myself? Let both of us go? Create an international incident? Why should they ever let us go? Yet even if they put us in prison, we would be alive. Martha would be alive. Innocence had not left me; my mind was locked into its framework of growing up prosperous and American. Even the bitter fruit of the depression had not touched Martha and me, and I kept rearranging this scene to fit my American-citizen-security mind. For the moment, I had stopped the process. Now I had to invent something that would satisfy them, and I tried desperately to pull out of my memory everything that Hollywood had made on Nazis, international intrigue, foreign agents, every book I could recall that dealt with such things. On shipboard, I had read a novel by Eric Ambler. I tried to remember it.

And Kreutzer waited quietly. I cleared my throat and began, "I don't know all the details—" I thought that was a good beginning, but Kreutzer held up his hand.

"One moment."

I swallowed my words and waited. Then the door opened, and Roldtmann entered, followed by a young woman with sharp features, an unsmiling mouth and glasses. She had pen and pad, and she took her place at the table. Roldtmann carried a pitcher of water and some paper cups. He poured a cup of water and handed it to me. I drank it.

"Now we begin," Kreutzer said. "Who enlisted you in this conspiracy? Start at the beginning."

"That damned old fool, my grandfather." I didn't know any other way to begin. Gramps was connected with Army Intelligence, according to what they told me. It made sense, and it couldn't do the old man any harm.

"How many others were involved?"

Careful here. Don't box yourself in. "There were a number of others—at least six. My wife was not involved. She had no idea of what was going on. Nothing. Absolutely."

"We will see."

"Who were the others? Name them, and give us their background."

"I can only name two of them." I scrounged my memory for

names. Horst—the Horst Wessel song, their national anthem. "Horst Bergmann—"

"Spell it."

I spelled it out. "And the other was Hans Schlieg." I spelled that name, trying to fix both names in my mind.

"Germans?"

I became more creative. I had known a boy at MIT who left school to fight in Spain against Franco. His action had fascinated me, I suppose because it was so unlikely in terms of my world.

"Horst Bergmann was German, yes. He was living in Paris. He had been a member of the German Brigade in the International, who were fighting against Franco." Don't get too complicated, I told myself. You can't just invent things. You have to remember what you invent. They're not fools.

"And Schlieg?"

"A German communist. That's all I know about him."

"They were the shooters," I said. "I suppose they felt it was better for me not to know any other names."

"The shooters who didn't shoot," Kreutzer said nastily. "Why didn't they shoot?"

"Because you grabbed Martha and me."

"The Fuhrer was immediately blocked by the guards. That could be the truth," he said to Kreutzer.

"Did you get the others, Bergmann and Schlieg? If you got them, then you know I'm telling the truth." Since both were inventions and did not exist, I was safe enough there.

Instead of answering my question, Kreutzer asked me what my role was. I had to explain the gun in my pocket.

"I was to be a diversion. If they succeeded in shooting Hitler, I was to create a diversion by shooting someone near me, anyone, but I don't think I could have gone through with it. I couldn't kill someone in cold blood."

The questioning went on and on, and I was getting in deeper and deeper, trying to keep the names and places I had invented in order. Finally, they ended it. I was hopeless now, grief-stricken, frightened, trying to keep from breaking down and bursting into tears. Nothing in my life had prepared me for this; and when I reflect upon my condition there and then, I realize that my upbringing, on my father's part, was an effort to make me the opposite of what he was, the opposite of the man who went up again and again in the silk and wire planes of World War One, risking his life in a manner inexplicable to me and beyond me.

Kreutzer and the stenographer left the room, leaving me with Roldtmann, who seated himself at the table and remained silent for the next half hour. I asked about Martha, where was she and when would I see her? No answer to that. I thought of leaping at him and trying to overpower him. They do that in film and books, but I had not the vaguest notion of how one goes about such a thing, and I felt that he had a gun somewhere on him, and the likelihood was that he could handle me without resorting to a gun, and in any case, the door was deadlocked. And they had Martha.

After half an hour, Kreutzer returned. "Hold out your hands," he said to me.

I held out my hands, and he took a pair of handcuffs out of his pocket and shackled my hands in front of me.

"Do you have the gun?" he asked Roldtmann.

Roldtmann took the Webley automatic out of his jacket pocket and handed it to him. Kreutzer dropped it into his jacket pocket. He then took Roldtmann over to a corner of the room and whispered to him. They whispered back and forth for a few minutes, and then Kreutzer said to me, "We're going now, Mr. Waring. Come along."

"When will I see my wife?"

"When we decide that you should see her, you will see her."

He went to the door, opened the deadlock with his key, and held the door open for me. I went through the door, and Roldtmann followed. We went downstairs, leaving Roldtmann behind. Kreutzer spoke quietly to a uniformed SS man. Then the three of us, Kreutzer, the SS man, and I between them, left the building. A large Mercedes four-door stood at the curb. The SS man opened the door, and Kreutzer and I got into the back. The SS man climbed in behind the wheel, and we drove off.

I asked where we were going. Kreutzer ignored the question.

# IV

*I*t was dark when I got into the car, and as we drove, through Berlin and out of Berlin, rain began to fall. We were on the *Autobahn,* one of the wide, four-lane roads that was Hitler's gift to German civilization. We drove for about two hours, and then we pulled off the *Autobahn* onto a side road and stopped at an inn of some kind. Kreutzer remained in the car with me, while the SS man went inside. He was gone for about ten minutes, and while he was gone, Kreutzer said to me, "If you want to piss, do it now."

"Where?"

"Just get out of the car and piss. It's dark and it's raining. You won't offend anyone."

I did as he said. I had not dealt very much with hate in my life up to this point. Brought up as I was, I found little reason to hate anything or anyone; and as far as Adolf Hitler and the Nazis were concerned, they were a sort of comic lot that strutted through the papers and newsreel film. Now I was learning to hate. I hated Germany; I hated Nazism; and above all, I hated Kreutzer. This was a new feeling for me, a hatred that was a cross between a sickness and some energizing drug. The SS man came back out of the inn carrying a cardboard carton. In it were three bottles of beer, half a dozen slices of dark bread, and some sliced sausage.

"Keep an eye on him," Kreutzer said, and left the car to do what I had done.

"Where did you learn your German, mister?" the SS man asked me. "It's pretty damn good."

"Wasted years in school."

"Unusual for an American," Kreutzer said, getting back into the car. "Of course, in your case, you were trained for your business."

"What business is that?"

"Assassination."

The SS man offered me some sausage and a slice of bread. "They make their own. It's good here."

"I'm not hungry."

Kreutzer took the bread and meat and began to eat. "He's right. It's a liver sausage. You probably never tasted anything like it in America. Try it."

I shook my head, but accepted the beer. My mouth was dry as leather. I was trying to deal with the probability that I might never see Martha again—indeed, I was coming to accept the fact that when they had gotten all they desired out of me in the way of information, they would kill me. My body would be found somewhere, the result of an accident, perhaps together with Martha's body. There would be international regrets. And if my cock-and-bull story did not hold up, as it probably would not, the next step would be torture. In any case, what there was of life and happiness for Scott Waring was over. I think I was as angry, sick and hopeless as any man could be.

"Where are you taking me?" I asked Kreutzer.

"To a place where certain people would like to meet you and hear your story."

"And then you kill me."

"Why should you think the worst of us? We have treated you decently."

"And of course, you treated my wife decently."

"We did what we had to do."

The rain increased. We were in wooded, hilly country now, and the rain was falling in sheets. A truck came zooming downhill on a blind bend of the road. This was no *Autobahn* but a two-lane macadam road, and the truck was almost in the middle. The SS man swerved to the right; the truck roared off into the night and the rain, and the SS man fought to control the car. I did the one positive thing I had done since this horror began. I raised my chained hands, leaned forward, and struck the driver on the back of his head with all my strength. I think I remember Kreutzer clutching at my arm, and then the driver lost control and the car skidded and lurched over the side of the road. I don't remember too clearly what happened after that. There was a slope on our right, down to a river. The car tore down the slope, lurching and rocking, the driver fighting to control it, Kreutzer struggling for his gun. Actually, it was the Webley he managed to pull out of his side pocket. All of this happened in a few seconds, so I am not very clear about the sequence of events, and I remember only a glimpse of the Webley. The driver had jammed on his brakes, and we skidded in what must have been wet mud, lifted, and then turned over in what appeared to be slow motion.

I was hitting at Kreutzer with my manacled hands, and I think he fired the Webley, and then we were in the river. But it was night and everything was black and I saw nothing, and the car was filling with water. I don't remember struggling with the door, but somehow I got it open. There was no movement from either Kreutzer or the SS man. I was choking for breath, I knew I was dying, and I was screaming inside of myself as I forced the door open, and then I was in the river and on the surface, taking great gulps of the night air. I was a fair swimmer, but it was hard with the hand-irons, and I was bruised and shaken and traumatized, but after a few feet of trying to swim and half drowning at the same time, I was able to stand and then make my way to the river's edge. It was May, but the water was icy cold. I dragged myself onto the river bank and lay there in the rain, shivering and whimpering in a kind of terror that would not leave me. I had crawled onto the bank no more than twenty or thirty feet from where the car went under, and I strained now to see whether any of it was visible and whether Kreutzer and the SS man would be coming after me, but I could see nothing and no one appeared out of the darkness.

So there I was, soaking wet, cold, manacled and frightened, in the middle of Germany or at least somewhere in Germany —for where I was I had not the vaguest notion—with neither hope nor direction. I knew one thing, that when daylight came, the Mercedes would be visible from the road, and that I had better not be where I was. I got to my feet and began to walk along the river bank. There was a muddy path that I could barely make out, and I must have followed it for perhaps a hundred yards when I came to a stone staircase. I rested for a few minutes, leaning against an iron railing, trying to think of some sensible thing to do and trying to overcome the trembling. I could think of nothing, so I climbed the staircase which ended at the road above.

I walked down the road. They had not taken my watch, and I tried to read it in the darkness, holding it close to my eyes. My watch had stopped, but that didn't matter. I couldn't read it in any case, and I learned later that I must have come out of the river at about three o'clock in the morning. I then walked down the road a bit. No car passed me, nothing stirred. And then, on the other side of the road, I saw the vague bulk of a house, a large, half-timbered structure. I stopped and waited and tried to think. I was so cold and tired and miserable and defeated that I was tempted to cross the road and hammer at the door of the house and give myself up for a cup of hot coffee and shelter from the rain, which was now only a drizzle but just as cold and uncomfortable as when it had poured down in torrents.

I crossed the road, and then I saw a small shed-like structure to one side and behind the house. At least it appeared to be a shed, and I decided that it was possibly a place to hide, and if it were a shed with tools, perhaps I could find something to break my shackles. None of this was thought out clearly. What I did was done because there were no alternatives that made any more sense. I stumbled and fell as I moved past the side of the house, and a dog began to bark. It was a shed, a flat roof over a pile of firewood, but I had shelter from the rain. That was all I had. I crouched against the piled firewood, shivered and surrendered myself to whatever awaited me.

As I write this, I think of all the books I have read and all the films I have seen where resourceful and intrepid men have worked or fought their way out of situations like mine. Possibly; but I was neither resourceful nor intrepid. I was frightened and hopeless, and when I heard a door in the house open and close, I did nothing, nor did my Congregationalist background inspire me to prayer. I simply remained where I was. I heard footsteps, and I saw a hand-held flashlight coming my way, and when the light was full on me, I did nothing. I was past running and there was no place for me to run to.

The man with the flashlight flicked it toward his other hand, which held a revolver. "Don't move," he said. "Just stay right where you are."

I didn't move.

"Stand up."

I stood up.

"Who are you? What do you want?" He saw the handcuffs. "Why are you shackled?"

"My name is Scott Waring," I said hopelessly. "I'm an American. I was picked up by the Gestapo. I was being transported in a car. The car went off the road, and I got out and they didn't. That's all. The car is in the river." I made it as simple as that. I had no recourse and I could think of no other explanation.

The man with the light held it on me, and the seconds ticked by and he said nothing and the light did not waver. At last he said, "What did you do?"

"Nothing."

"Of course, nothing. All right, come out of there and walk where I point the light. If you want to run, then run. I won't shoot you and I won't stop you."

"I have no place to run."

"Then come with me, and follow the light."

He pointed the light, and I walked with the circle of illumination to the house.

"Stand right there," he said. He opened a door at the back of the house, and switched on a light. In the light that poured out of the doorway, I saw him for the first time, a slender young man who could have been no more than sixteen or seventeen, dark hair, brown eyes, an untroubled, self-confident face. "Come inside," he said, still covering me with his revolver. I was in the kitchen of the house, a large, modern kitchen with a tile floor and an enormous refrigerator. In the center, there was a large work table, thick butcher-block wood. The boy pointed to a chair. "Sit down, Herr American." I dropped gratefully into a chair. "Your German is very good," he said. "But the accent is English, so you could be an American, I suppose. I don't believe you did nothing. The Gestapo is very gifted in their trade."

"Where are we? Where is this?"

"A few miles from Coburg. The Gestapo has an operational house there."

"Are you going to turn me over to them?" I glanced down at the floor, where a puddle was forming from my wet clothes. He noticed my look and he went to a closet and took out a towel and handed it to me.

At that moment, the door at the other end of the kitchen opened and a woman wrapped in a quilted silk robe entered. She was a large, buxom woman, about fifty, I guessed, dyed blond hair gathered at the back of her neck, dark-eyed, with a certain commanding air about her, even at this hour of the morning. She had apparently just awakened, possibly from the barking of the dog.

"What the devil goes on here?" she demanded. "Who's that?"

"He's an American. What did you say your name is?" he asked me.

"Scott Waring."

"Ah-hah. Scott Waring."

The young man now repeated to the woman everything I had told him, and while she listened, she never took her eyes off me. I had a feeling that those eyes were undressing me, opening my mind, taking each part of me apart and analyzing me.

"Take off that jacket!" she said sharply, and to the boy, "Paul, can't you see he's shivering. It's bad enough to have him here; to have him here with a case of pneumonia is more than we need. Get him some clothes. First take a knife and cut the sleeves."

"Mine won't fit him."

"Oh, stupid. Take some that Colonel Schturm leaves. He'll never know the difference." Paul went off to get Colonel Schturm's clothes, and I began to believe that somewhere I had left reality behind and this was part of a continuing nightmare.

"Get out of those wet clothes," she said to me, taking the knife the boy had used and cutting my shirt away from my body.

"Here?"

"Not here, stupid." The term of address, *Dummkopf,* was evidently a favorite of hers. "Over by the stove, where it's warm." She was to be obeyed. One didn't argue with her. I began to undress—and then paused in my underclothes.

"Don't be a fool. Take off your clothes. Don't be modest here. This is a whorehouse, a house of prostitution." At first the word eluded me; *Dirne* may have been the word, or perhaps something else. It was not in my German vocabulary. "This is my house, I am the madam *(gnädige Frau),*" as she put it. "Do you understand? Your prick will not upset me. I deal with the worst pricks in the Fatherland."

She opened a drawer and took out pliers, screw driver, and a set of metal clippers. Quickly and expertly—as I imagine she did everything—she bent and snapped the shackles. Paul returned with an armful of the Colonel's clothes, socks, trousers, a woolen shirt and a tweed jacket. "His shoes wouldn't fit you," Paul said. "Yours will dry."

The madam—her name, I learned, was Berthe Baum—had poured a cup of coffee. She sliced bread and a thick slice of ham, and motioned for me to sit at the table and eat. Paul still had his gun on me.

"Oh, put away that stupid gun. And you, Herr Waring, you tell me everything and no bullshit."

I ate and drank ravenously and somehow talked at the same time. I told her everything, who I was, why Martha and I were in Germany, and all that had happened to bring me here. When I had finished, her attitude changed.

"Poor bastard," she said, "poor, stupid American bastard."

"Are you going to turn me in?"

"What do you think?"

"Then why are you helping me?"

"Listen to me, Herr Waring. Paul here is my son. I am Jewish. Do you imagine you hate the SS? You don't know the meaning of hate. I exist because I run a whorehouse, and because those pigs patronize my girls, and because I have enough on each and every one of them. They know that. They need me, and I need them, because there is no other way for me, as a Jew, to exist in the Fatherland. Maybe a God I don't believe in brought you here, maybe luck. But I would help you if only to deny them the satisfaction of beating you to death. You have heard about the Gestapo and torture, fancy torture? No. They beat people to death. They love it. They love to break bones and tear flesh. It feeds what they call their Aryan manliness. Then they come to me and fuck my girls, or they drink my beer and weep over their impotence, or they fuck each other or the little boys they bring with them. Now, from what you tell me, the car will be discovered as soon as it is light. Then they will be all over this house and every other house between here and Coburg. So here is what you are going to do. There is a train to Berlin that stops at Coburg at seven o'clock. Paul will take you to the station, and you will buy a ticket to Berlin. In Berlin at the station, take a taxicab to the American Embassy. You must move quickly and boldly, and with a little luck, we will get away clean, both of us. The search for you will be here, not in Berlin, and it may be hours before they pull the car out of the river and work out the situation."

"They took my wallet. I have no money."

"I'll give you enough. I will die with the money I have."

My eyes filled with tears as I kissed her and embraced her. She gave me three hundred marks, and laughed when I said I would send the money back to her.

"Use it and bribe the moment an occasion arises. They are easy to bribe. And don't send anything back to me. I don't need any letters or money from America, and if you ever reach that *goyisha* heaven of yours, put in a word for a Jewish lady in hell. Now go and be bold, not careful."

Her son, Paul, drove me to the station, timing it carefully so that we arrived only ten minutes before the Berlin train pulled into Coburg. I bought my ticket, taking a whole compartment, as she had suggested, and then sat back to watch the countryside drift by. It was impossible and incredible, but here I was, dry, my stomach full, filled with some childish conviction that Martha would be waiting for me. I fell asleep. The conductor awakened me to tell me that we would be in Berlin in a few minutes.

# V

*N*othing dangerous or disturbing happened to me between Coburg and Berlin. I talked myself into believing that since I had come through alive and unharmed, except for a few cuts and bruises on my wrists, the same would be the fate of Martha. I could not believe otherwise or cope with the possibility that she was dead or that I would not see her again. Only twenty-four hours ago, we were walking hand in hand through the Tiergarten. I could feel the warmth of her flesh and hear the sound of her voice. During all the time I had known Martha, I could never answer the question of what she saw in me. She was brighter than I, certainly wittier, more alive in her response to every situation. Yet she had chosen me.

There was no brushing aside the fact that I was responsible for what had happened to both of us. I put that abominable Webley automatic in my pocket; I precipitated the situation that had developed over the past twenty-four hours, and for that I would never forgive myself.

But now I was in a normal course of events. Possibly the car had not yet been found; possibly the search was concentrated in Coburg; possibly the Gestapo was not quite as all-powerful and all-seeing as its reputation held it to be. In any case, I left my compartment and got off the train, trying to control myself and appear perfectly casual with my heart hammering away like some wild machine. I walked through the station, hailed a cab on the street outside, and told the driver to take me to the Embassy.

The rain had stopped; the sky was blue, and it was as mild and delightful a day in May as Berlin had ever seen. A policeman was directing traffic, precisely and expertly, as only a German policeman could. People strolled on the streets and children played, and altogether it was difficult to believe that beneath all this, a crazed, racist government was preparing to launch the greatest catastrophe the world had ever known. Had it actually happened? Had I been driven through the night in a blinding rainstorm? Had my life been saved by a Jewish madam who ran a brothel outside of Coburg?

A marine stopped me at the gate to the Embassy compound, and I identified myself as an American. He asked to see my passport, and when I explained that it was lost—actually in the hotel safe at the Adlon—he picked up his telephone, gave my name to the person at the other end and then looked at me curiously. "They said for you to go right in, Mr. Waring. Ask for Leonard Cutter. Mr. Cutter is the chargé d'affaires while the Ambassador is in Washington. He is expecting you."

I went into the Embassy. So Mr. Leonard Cutter was expecting me! That could only be because Martha had gotten to
the Embassy somehow and had told them the story of what
had happened. All my depression washed away, and the first
thing I said as I was ushered into Cutter's office was, "My
wife, Martha Waring, is she here?"

Cutter, a man in his fifties, carefully dressed, carefully spoken, rose as I entered the room, came around his desk and
shook hands with me. Then, instead of answering my question, he looked at me with a kind of desperation.

"My wife!" I said.

"Please sit down, Mr. Waring."

I didn't sit down. I grasped his arm and said, "For Christ's
sake, what happened to her?"

He shook his head. "There's no other way to tell you this.
I'm sorry. Your wife is dead. Her body was found early this
morning in Schloss-garten. Apparently, she was assaulted and
killed."

There is no way to write or describe what I felt at that
moment. The world simply ended. Everything ended. I have
heard that people who marry out of a fervent love might
continue to love each other as the years go by, but differently
than the initial passion, more quietly. I never experienced
that. My love for Martha was the utter adoration of first love, an
adoration never tested by living or working or suffering together. It was pure and romantic and apart from reality, and
while the past twenty-four hours were a kind of deadly coming of

age for one Scott Waring, it changed nothing in his love for the woman who had been his bride for less than two weeks.

I learned finality. Martha was dead, and deep down from the time I had seen her being beaten at Gestapo headquarters, I had known that I would not see her again. All the rest was illusion, all the hopes, all the fantasies. Now, reality.

I was staring past Cutter's desk at the two American flags that flanked it, and after a moment I realized that tears were running down my cheeks. Cutter handed me a handkerchief.

"Sit down, please, Mr. Waring," Cutter said. "We must talk and you must answer some questions. We only received word from the police half an hour ago. We have not yet spoken to anyone in the States. I wish to God the Ambassador were here, but he isn't and somehow I have to work this out on my own. Can I get you a drink? Coffee?"

"A little water," I managed to whisper.

He poured some from a jug on his desk. My hand shook so it splashed water on my trousers.

"Now," he said, "I would be very grateful to hear what you can tell me about this awful tragedy."

"Was she—was she raped?"

"I don't know that yet. I don't know anything except that the police found her body."

"How do they know it was my wife?"

"The identification was in her handbag. Any money she might have been carrying was gone, any jewels. Even her wedding band—she did have one, didn't she?"

I nodded.

"Do you feel up to talking?" he asked me.

"I'll try."

"And would you object if I were to have a stenographer take notes? I think your explanation might be very important."

I had no objection to that, and Cutter called in a stenographer, an American woman working in the Embassy. I then told Cutter everything that had happened to me during the past twenty-four hours. When I had finished, I said, "I trust you'll protect the name and place of this woman who saved my life."

"Of course." And to the stenographer, "Only one copy of that. No carbon. And when you've typed it out, bring me both your shorthand notes and the typed transcript."

"I understand," she agreed.

"And hold all my calls," Cutter told her, "except from Stateside." When she had left, he turned to me and said, "We have a problem—no, two problems."

I was in a state of shock, and thinking none too clearly. "You believe me?"

"Mr. Waring," he said, "of course I believe you. We were informed that you and your wife would be in Berlin at the Adlon. I know who your father is and I know who your grandfather is, and as a matter of fact, there is an invitation at the Adlon for you and your wife to join my wife and me at dinner tonight. It is hard to believe that the Gestapo could have been so inept and stupid, but paranoia breeds that, and this is a paranoid country, believe me. Is there anything you haven't told me?"

I shook my head dumbly, and then I remembered Wolf Horstmann, our shipboard table companion.

"Horstmann—yes, there's been talk about him. You know, Mr. Waring, after hearing what you've been through, I have no desire to quiz you. I think you should be alone with your grief. But we must act, and as I said, there are two problems. The first is the story you invented to save your wife. They may well have recorded that. The second is that only you can identify your wife's body. They have her body at the morgue at police headquarters, and unless we can get some satisfaction, I can't allow you to go there and subject yourself to another arrest by the Gestapo. I have some thoughts about that. Now I am going to take you upstairs and introduce you to my wife, and you can be alone for a while, and I'll see what might be done."

I nodded.

"I'll send to the Adlon for your clothes."

Mrs. Cutter, a grey-haired matronly woman, was more than kind to me. She gave me one of her husband's robes and a pair of slippers, suggested that I shower, and that when I finished showering and shaving, I might have tea and some sandwiches. She said that I might want to lie down for a while. In the guest room, I found towels, razor, toothbrush, all that I required; and after I had showered and shaved, I wrapped myself in the robe and lay down on the bed—all of this mechanically, feeling like a robot, shorn of all sensation and feeling. I must have fallen asleep immediately. When I awakened, coming out of a dream of sheer horror, I lay there weeping. The sun was setting. I must have been asleep for several hours.

There was a tap on the door, and then Mrs. Cutter came into the room. My luggage had been put in the room while I slept. Mrs. Cutter suggested that I dress and come downstairs as soon as possible. "I know how you must feel," she said, "and I wish you didn't have to talk about this. But Leonard is in his office with the Chief of Police, and I'm afraid you must talk to them."

I dressed, clean laundry, a tie and shirt and jacket and dry shoes. Mrs. Cutter was waiting as I came out of my room, and she took me downstairs to her husband's office. Inside, with Cutter, there was a stout, grim-faced man who was intro- duced to me as Herr Fliedens, the Chief of Police.

"Mine English is not goot," he said.

"We'll speak German," Cutter said. "Mr. Waring's German is quite good." He turned to me. "I have repeated to Herr Fliedens the gist of what you told me. He would like to ask you some questions."

"In particular," Fliedens said, "what happened when the car you say you were riding in went into the river?"

I told him how I had escaped.

"The accident has been reported," he said. "There was no mention of a passenger in the car, only Herr Kreutzer and Lieutenant Guttmann."

I shrugged.

"Where were you when your wife—if it is your wife—was attacked?"

"I don't know when she died, but when she was attacked, I was in Gestapo headquarters, watching two of your thugs beat a harmless woman into unconsciousness."

"For which we have only your word."

"A man named Roldtmann was there."

"You say that someone in Coburg helped you to get back to Berlin and removed your hand-irons. Who was it?"

"I have no intentions of telling you," I said.

"Then you will be in worse trouble, Herr Waring, believe me."

"No, sir," Cutter said. "I would like you to consider, Herr Fliedens, who will be in trouble. I have already informed Washington of this incident. At the moment, Mr. Hitler will bend over backwards not to offend my government. Perhaps you can visualize the headlines in the *New York Herald Tribune,* **Gestapo Brutally Murders American Bride.** I can imagine how that would please Herr Goebbels. Show him your wrists, please, Mr. Waring."

Pulling back my sleeves, I showed him my wrists, scratched and bruised.

"Americans are a very emotional people, Herr Fliedens. The story of what happened to the Warings would sweep the country. There is already a strong feeling about the Nazi Party and its iniquities."

Fliedens thought about that, and for a minute or two, the three of us sat in silence. Then he said, "What do you want? I am a policeman. I am not the Gestapo."

"Understand, I am not speaking for myself. As you know, I am not the ambassador. But I have been in touch with Washington, and they are very plain about what they want. In the first place, no further action is to be taken against Scott Waring. He must have the right to leave the country without hindrance. All of his and his wife's possessions must be returned to him, including a diamond bracelet taken from his wife. And the Gestapo agents must be publicly identified and brought to trial."

"Two of them are dead, drowned."

"Roldtmann is not dead."

"I told you. I am only a policeman. I do not make policy."

"Then you will clear this with those who do make policy. Further, Mr. Waring must go to the morgue and identify the body of the woman who was murdered. He is not to be interfered with or arrested. I shall send him in an Embassy car with armed guards. If any attempt against him is made, we will resist and you will have an international incident of major proportions, and I do not have to elaborate on what such an incident can lead to. As we say in my country, you have a very hot potato on your hands. We will do this tonight."

As before, Fliedens was silent, and minutes went by while we sat silently and watched him. Then, finally, he nodded and asked for a telephone where he could speak privately. Cutter escorted him from the room and then returned.

"I think this will work," he said.

Somewhere inside of me was a small grain of hope that the body would not be Martha—a very small grain of hope. About ten minutes went by. Cutter told me that he had spoken to my father. "That was while you slept," he explained. "He asked that you telephone him after we see your wife's body."

Cutter's wife entered the office, leading a man who carried a tray with tea and sandwiches. He opened a folding table, and set down the food. Cutter poured tea and offered me a sandwich. I shook my head. Mrs. Cutter and the servant left, and then Cutter and I sat and waited, making no real effort to talk. Another ten minutes or so went past.

"Time enough for him to reach the top," Cutter said.

Ten minutes more, and then Cutter said, "Time enough. I'll get him."

Then I sat in the office alone, staring at the clock on Cutter's desk, and trying to make some sense out of life and my future. Then Cutter returned with Fliedens, and the Chief of Police said to me, "I am a policeman, Herr Waring. I was a policeman ten years before Herr Hitler became chancellor. I am not the Gestapo. As I have already told Herr Cutter, no action will be taken against you. You have my word on that and you have Herr Goebbels's word. The proper action will be taken against Roldtmann, and apologies will be made. We can go to the morgue now, and, as Herr Cutter suggested, I will go with you. There is no need for an armed guard."

I looked at Cutter, and he nodded.

The morgue was in the basement of a large, somber building. Perhaps it was police headquarters. I didn't inquire. We went down a flight of stairs, Cutter, Fliedens and myself, into a large brightly lit room that stank of formaldehyde, making our way through white tile dissecting tables to a body refrigerator that occupied an entire wall. An attendant pulled out one of the body drawers and uncovered the body.

I walked over and stared at it. Then I reached out and touched her cheek. It was as cold as ice. Her body was naked, her hair gathered behind her head, her face bruised and purple where she had been struck. I bent and kissed her lips. I was crying now, not sobbing or hysterical, but simply crying as I had not cried since I was a small child, not as I had cried a few hours before, but as a helpless child cries.

Cutter drew me away. I dried my eyes. "I'm sorry," I said to Cutter. Strangely, I was ashamed for the Germans to see my tears. The pathologist on duty joined us, and Cutter asked softly, "How did she die? What killed her?"

"Her skull was fractured. A cranial hemorrhage. We won't know until I do the autopsy . . ."

"No autopsy!" I cried violently. "There will be no autopsy! Cover her!" I shouted at the attendant. "I want her body sent home the way it is! I don't want her embalmed and I don't want her body touched."

"As you wish," Fliedens said.

"Let's get out of here," Cutter said. "I'll take care of everything. There will be no autopsy."

If they are nothing else, they are efficient. Martha's body went with me on the same train to Cherbourg, where we went on board the *Queen Mary* once again. As we had sailed to Europe, so did Martha and I return to America, except that Martha lay in a sealed coffin in the ship's hold and I took my meals alone at a small table, where I was spared condolences or any other conversation. Captain MacGregor was kind and considerate, but I was not looking for commiseration. I wanted only to be left alone, and I begged him not to make my story a matter of ship gossip. A bright-eyed, happy young man had gone to Europe and had surrendered his youth there.

# VI

*I* had never been to the funeral of someone close to me, and as I stood in the cemetery of the Congregational church in Connecticut where the Pembrokes had their summer home, I was without any feeling of prayer or faith. Martha was gone. The words of the pastor were meaningless to me. Martha was dead. All the world had been mine, and now nothing was mine; and I stood like an empty shell while Martha's coffin was lowered into the earth.

And still it was the month of May, in 1939, the month that had seen us married, and now it was the 31st of May, and in 25 days I had crossed the Atlantic twice, and for 11 of those days, I had lived with the woman I made my wife. I had used up all my emotion, all my volatile response, all my ability to register grief. Martha's mother stood next to me and wept. I wanted to hold her and tell her how bright and wonderful her daughter had been, but I was too empty for that. Mr. Pembroke took her hand and led her away. My sister, Linda, threw her arms around me. "Scott, I understand." But I was alive, while Martha was dead. Everyone wore black or some dark color. This was ritual, the survival of ancient funerary rites. My mother kissed me and said, "She is with God now," and voiceless, I replied, No, she is in that cold, damp earth. The God who created Adolf Hitler and Nazi Germany has no place for Martha Waring.

There is nothing more bloodless than a white Protestant funeral in families that have several generations of proper manners behind them. In the years since then, I have been to Irish wakes, where the mourners ate food, drank whisky and spoke praise of the deceased; to Jewish funerals where the women wept and wailed; to Italian funerals where the women threw themselves on the coffin, moaning and wailing. But at this funeral there were only quiet tears and gentle sympathy. I would have preferred screams of sorrow and anger and curses flung at the men who did this. I felt that I was alone in my rage that the various Pembrokes and Warings gathered there in the Pembroke living room after the funeral were removed from all such tribal matters. When I mentioned this to my father, later that evening, he observed that perhaps they felt it very deeply indeed, that they had not surrendered the feeling but only the power to express it.

It was after midnight, back in our apartment in New York City, and I had gone to bed, trying to sleep and unable to sleep. I put on a robe and slippers and went into my father's study. He was staying here overnight, and in the morning, he would return to Washington.

My father was not an easily articulate man. He was forty-four at this time, his hair gone grey, a tall, thin, mild-mannered man, slow to speak unless it was on the single subject that had consumed so much of his life, airplanes. Now, he was sitting in his favorite chair, a newspaper on his lap. "Can't sleep," I explained, and dropped into a chair alongside. "Is Mother all right?"

"She has lived through all that happened to you. That's too much imagination. She took a sleeping pill. She'll be all right. You know, she loved Martha. We all did."

"And you?" I asked him.

He evaded the question and noted that this was the first time today that he had been able to look at the newspapers. The fact of the matter was that he had cancer, and that three years later, he would be dead. "Part of my job, I suppose, knowing what goes on in this miserable world." He tapped the newspapers. "Here it is—Cordell Hull calling for the repeal of the arms embargo—which as much as says to France and England, take a stand. We'll support you. If they had only done it two months ago, Czechoslovakia might have survived. Hull is right, and now if the President can only shake loose from that crowd of brain-damaged isolationists, we may still be in time."

"Then you think there'll be war?"

He poured a glass of brandy for me, and then for himself. Sharing a cigar with my father was a measure of communion that I treasured. He offered the box to me now, and we both made our selections and lit up, and for the first time since I saw Martha beaten through that one-way mirror at Gestapo headquarters, I was able to relax a bit, to begin to accept the fact that I had to go on living in this world.

"Will there be war?" my father said. "There is war—there was war from the day Adolf Hitler marched into Austria. Then the Czechs. Next—Poland, I suppose, and after that, God only knows."

"It's not a pleasant picture."

He winced and grimaced with pain. The pain was in his side. I don't know whether it was the cancer, but his was not an easy stomach. Neither of us knew how ill he actually was.

"I have been trying to think of how I could talk to you about Martha?" It came out as a sort of question. We had never had the so-called man-to-man relationship that exists between some fathers and their sons. He knew how I felt about war and the military thread that ran through our family and his passion to design a fighting plane that was better and faster than anything any other nation had. There was a brief period when, as a teenager, I became a vegetarian. He had accepted it then, but not without a streak of disdain; yet he had never allowed my hatred of war to really come between us.

I watched the smoke of my cigar for a few moments, and then I said, "We don't have to talk about Martha."

"With all due respect for your feelings and your pain, I think you do have to talk about Martha. You have gone through a rough passage, and you're a different person than you were a month ago. You have been vetted, as the British say, torn apart and not yet put together. You loved and you lost—but don't lose Martha. Talk about her. Remember her."

"I remember her."

"You had a gift, even if a very small and agonizing one, but you did have a gift, the gift of a wonderful young woman, and in the time between your first knowing her and then losing her, you had what few men have. That's a gift, if you understand what I mean."

I thought about it for a little while before I answered. "I think I know what you mean. Maybe, some day, I'll be able to look at it as you suggest. Not now."

He nodded, and then we sat in silence for a few minutes, smoking our cigars. And then I said, "Have you ever thought about why there are wars?"

"I've thought about it. Scott," he said, his tone changing, "I want you to do something for me."

"Anything I can do."

"I want you to go back to school in the fall and get your degree. There is going to be a war, and we are going to be drawn into it. If you are drawn into it, you will have a commission in the Engineers—if you want it."

"I won't want it."

"We'll see," he said gently. "Things change."

"Yes, I suppose so."

"And will you go back to school?"

"I'll think about it."

In the end, I did go back to MIT. I still wanted to be an engineer and to build bridges. That was one of the very few things I wanted. We had a summer place on Saranac Lake in the Adirondacks, but it was a place filled with the memories of a summer month when Martha came to stay with us, and I could not face the thought of being there. Instead, I found a job with Holben-Chute, a large engineering firm. Two years ago, an engineering student might have paced the streets of New York for months without finding a place that would hire him. But everything was changing now that we were shifting into a war economy, and jobs became available almost overnight. Mine was nothing very important. I sat over a drawing board from nine to five, or when the occasion demanded, from nine to nine. Our house at Saranac had been rented and my mother was with my father in Washington. I had the apartment to myself, and since most of our friends were out of town for the summer months, I was not put in the position of declining dinner invitations. The story of what had happened to Martha and me did not hit the press, the silence being a part of the agreement that took me out of Germany, and while people in the family knew more or less of what had happened, they did not bruit it around. I preferred it that way.

The summer was tedious, lonely and hot. There were opportunities to meet girls, and there were some very attractive women who worked at the same company, but girls were the

last thing I desired in those few months after Martha's death.
I traced drawings and blueprints and made the changes I was
told to make. I even dared to show my department head some
of my own drawings, and I was congratulated for being creative, but I was still being a gofer, sent out for lunch-time
coffee and sandwiches. I was paid $30.00 a week, which was a
very decent wage for a college student on a summer job. I
visited my folks in Washington twice on weekends, and once
I went to Connecticut to spend a weekend with the Pembrokes, who were kind and loving and who felt that through
me they could touch something of their daughter. My sister,
Linda, was married to John Farraday, vice-president at the
City Federal Bank and part of what New York still called
society. She had me to dinner once, and I listened silently and
with considerable disgust to John and his friends cursing
Franklin Delano Roosevelt and insisting that we could do
business with Hitler, and that he had brought prosperity and
stability to Germany. Linda was embarrassed and unhappy,
but she had promised that no word of my experience would
be spoken, and she stuck to her word. It would be 1947,
eight years later, before I would again be a guest at her dinner table, but I will get to that in due time.

Then, in September, I went back to the Massachusetts Institute of Technology to complete my senior year. Other
things happened in that month of September, 1939, and I
refer to them briefly in order to frame this narrative in a very
important historical background:

On the first day of September, the Nazi armies swept into Poland, brutally crushing any resistance. Two days later, Britain and France declared war on Germany, and on the 17th of that month, Russian troops invaded Poland from the east. On the 10th of September, a British expeditionary force began to land in France, and by the 18th of that month, German U-boats had sunk 20 British ships, including an aircraft carrier. So began the horror of World War Two.

That last year at MIT was very different from my junior year. In the past, students would discuss the problem of jobs in a depression-stricken land; now war had begun, and it was less a question of jobs than the United States Army versus civilian life. Actually, no one really believed that we could sit out the war, and in a technical college, Britain's condition of unpreparedness was only too well understood. And then, in May, only a year since Martha and I had set out on our honeymoon, the disaster of Dunkirk took place.

It was at that time, before the graduation exercises, that Professor Hans Bauman approached me with a proposal—which strangely enough determined much that would happen to me, not in terms of the conversation I had with him at the time, but in terms of a shared effort still well in the future. It was my relationship to him that changed, from teacher and student to two men who came to know and trust each other.

Professor Bauman was forty-three at the time, a short, stocky man with a close-cropped beard and a pair of piercing blue eyes. He was Jewish. In 1935, in Berlin, where he and his wife both taught at Friedrich-Wilhelm University, his wife had been arrested on suspicion of being a communist. At the same time, he was fired from his teaching post. He never again saw his wife after her arrest, and what he could find out indicated that she, like Martha, had been beaten to death by the Gestapo. He managed to leave Germany, and he was taken on the faculty of MIT. Somehow, possibly from the president of the school—who did know my story—he learned the details of what had happened to me. I often suspected that giving him the information was an attempt to help me, and indeed Professor Bauman and I had a number of discussions about Germany, the Nazi movement, and the handling of personal grief.

In his field, Stress and Structure, Professor Bauman was recognized as a singular authority. He had written a definitive work on the molecular structure of metals, and he had independently discovered and put into use in Europe the theory of indeterminacy that had made the George Washington Bridge possible. Thus, when he made the proposal to me in May of 1940, we were already on reasonably intimate terms.

He began by asking me whether I had any firm post-graduate plans, and I told him that Holben-Chute, for whom I had worked this past summer, had already offered me a job at five thousand a year.

"They don't build bridges," he said.

"Yes, I know. That's why I haven't accepted—as yet."

"I know how you feel about war," Professor Bauman said.

"As far as the philosophy of pacifism is concerned, I could not agree with you more. But at this moment, in this year of 1940, pacifism becomes almost impossible."

"It's a personal thing. For myself, it always has been. I grew up in a warm and loving family, but it was a military family, and even when I was a kid, my life only made sense in terms of a hatred of war."

"Of course, considering your situation."

"No—perhaps some of it was resistance to what they believed. But more of it was the development of my own thinking. You see, sir, for myself—well, I could not kill another human being, regardless of the provocation."

"To save your own life?"

"I don't know," I answered slowly.

"But you did kill two men to save your own life."

We were walking in the Common, and while I was listening to Hans Bauman and replying to his questions, it was all mechanical and my mind was with the sunny May day and the tranquility of the Common, the young wives wheeling prams, the children playing and the swans strutting at the edge of the pond. His softly spoken accusation took me aback.

"Albeit, you might not have intended their deaths."

"Two men." For the moment I had not the vaguest notion of what he meant.

"In the car—the man whose name you said was Kreutzer, and the SS man."

"I didn't mean to kill them."

"Oh?"

We walked on and I thought about it and took myself back to that night when we drove through the teeming rain to Coburg. "I meant to kill them," I finally admitted. "But it could have been all three of us. It's hard for me to explain how frightened I was."

"You don't have to explain," Bauman said. "I know the feeling. You know, my wife was not a communist. I was not a communist. I don't even know whether they really suspected that she was. They interrogated her and she died."

"Yes."

"What does this lead up to, Scott? I was offered a commission last week in the Army Corps of Engineers. The job is to teach the practical building of bridges. To make a kind of pun, as you say in English, there will be many bridges to cross before this war is over, and there will be many bridges to destroy. Build some and destroy others, but we call it civilization."

"And you accepted?"

"Of course. This country has been good to me. It gave me life and it gave me refuge. What a strange quandary for me, to love Germany as much as I love Germany, and to hate the Nazis as much as I hate them. Today I am Major Hans Bauman of the Army Corps of Engineers. I wanted an assistant, I told them, a brilliant student of mine who is also fluent in German. You have no idea how much weight that carries.

This country has no army to speak of, only a few thousand men. So if you wish, I will give you the papers to sign, and you can come with me to take the oath. It's very informal. This is not a military country. You will be commissioned a lieutenant."

"If I agree."

"Scott, we will not be training people to kill. We will be training them to build bridges."

"And to destroy them."

"Yes. When the need arises."

"Can I have a day or two to think about it?"

"Of course."

When I look back now, my life appears to have been arranged as a sort of jigsaw puzzle, handed to me piece by piece, for me to set into place; and I ask myself, as I have a hundred times, did it begin with the Webley automatic that my gun-crazed grandfather bestowed upon me, or was it all a matter of chance and is all life and all the universe a kind of chaos that physicists discuss today? And speaking of the Webley, a package arrived from the Berlin police a few weeks after I had returned to America, and there, together with Martha's bag and diamond bracelet and wedding ring, was my wallet and the Webley.

Yet I am more ready to believe that the series of events that I narrate here would have been more or less the same—regardless of the Webley.

I think I knew from the moment Hans Bauman broached

the matter to me that in the end I would agree to accept the commission. For one thing, the pattern of my life during that whole school year was one of boredom and separateness. It seemed to me that I was a dozen years older than my class-mates. The senior year in a college is the rutting season, the pairing off by the steadier youngsters and the mad rush to score by those who could not cope with a single partner. I was an outsider. I couldn't play their games and the women left me cold. I am sure I was subject to a lasting trauma, and the promise of playing a role in this great confusion that was beginning to envelop the world overcame my hatred of vio-lence. In a sense, both the army and the navy are security chambers of a certain kind. Each day is arranged; clothes are given to you and meals are served to you—and it may be that such a situation was exactly what I needed.

I wrote to my father, telling him what I intended to do. After some personal matters, I wrote, "This decision on my part will surprise you, yet I don't think you will be upset. I have been offered a commission in the Army Corps of Engi-neers, and I have accepted it, and I will have the beginning rank of second lieutenant. They appear to be quite desperate for certain skilled help, and the officers I spoke with fairly jumped with delight at my facility with the German lan-guage." I did not attempt further explanation. But two months later, I wrote, "So far, everything I have encountered has been enveloped in total confusion, and how they will ever put this together and turn it into an effective army, I can't imagine. I had two or three lectures in school on pontoon bridging, which just dented my ignorance. I have been reading like mad, and the major and I—that's Hans—have been flying all over the country from army base to army base and to Fort this and Fort that to look at their bridging equipment—most of which is simply not usable. The blueprints pile up as we try to work out basic units for manufacture, and we have devised basic units out of balsa wood for the engineering teams to practice with. They are cheap and easily produced. In all truth this has been good medicine for me, since I have been busy morning to night with no time to brood and remember.

"Oddly, and this may shock you, I am proud of the fact that my country is as ill-prepared for war as any country in the world. We are, thank God, a nation of peace, and so far nothing much seems to be changing that fact. Tell Mother not to worry. The worst danger I encountered was about five days of some kind of basic training. And I am getting over my fear of flying. The next time you ask me to go up with you, I won't refuse. The basic training was cut short because they were building a new army base in Georgia and they needed a quick bridge for their trucks."

So much for that moment in my life. All too soon, we became a nation of war.

# Part Two

# New York

# I

*L*ast night, I dreamed about Martha. I dreamed that Martha and I were walking along a river-bank. Or possibly a lake, because it was almost solid with lily pads. I was trying to remember to tell her something—in the dream, I mean—" I saw his face, and I paused. It was at my request that we sat facing each other, and he had assented readily enough.

"I don't think we should talk about Martha today," Dr. Lieberman said.

"Why?"

"It hasn't proved profitable. I think it's a diversion, consciously or unconsciously."

"I don't agree."

"You don't agree. But consider. Martha has been dead for twelve years. The death of a partner in a good marriage is certainly one of the most savage traumas a human being must endure. But you were married a very short time, and twelve years have passed. It is common for a newly widowed partner in a marriage to fall into the belief that a husband or wife has left and will return. You may consider me unfeeling because again and again I have turned you away from this fantasy. Martha is dead. Martha will not return. The dead do not return. People die. You will die. I will die. It is pointless and unprofitable for us to talk about Martha. We have talked a great deal about Martha. I want to find another path."

"To what?"

"To your pain. You know what obsession is?"

"Sort of—I guess."

"It derives," Dr. Lieberman said, "from the ancient notion of possession, a person seized by an evil spirit. We try to think of it more scientifically, if you will, a creation or a response of the mind that blocks or replaces other traumas. Not that such an explanation means much more than the old idea of possession."

I thought about that for a while, and he waited patiently. He was a tall, thin man in his middle fifties, partially bald and nearsighted. He wore gold-rimmed glasses, and his blue eyes were large and liquid, as is often the case with near-sighted people. In his office, he usually wore brown duck trousers or blue jeans, and a dark sweatshirt. He was an M.D., and during the war he had worked as a surgeon in an army hospital in England, an experience which, as he once told me, had turned him to psychiatry.

"Of course," he said, breaking the silence, "we all suffer from obsession, some of it small and of little consequence, some of it destructive. In my case, it was blood, the sight and thought of it, one of the reasons I gave up surgery."

"Could you have cured yourself?"

He shrugged. "Let's not get off on that. Suppose we talk about Buchenwald."

"No."

"Why not?"

"You know why not. Anyway, I haven't dreamed about Buchenwald in weeks. Last night, I dreamed about Martha. Aren't we supposed to work on dreams?"

"Let me be the doctor. By the way, how do you feel about Jews?"

"Jews?"

"Yes, Jews. I'm Jewish, as you might have guessed. I'm asking you how you feel about Jews?"

I shook my head hopelessly. "I don't feel about Jews. They're people."

"That's nicely put. Do you have Jewish friends?"

I was becoming increasingly irritated. My take-home pay as consulting design engineer on a bridge that was being built in Westchester County was six hundred and some odd dollars a week, almost half of which went to Dr. Lieberman. It is true that he made special time for me when it rained or snowed and work was halted, but this thing about Jews put me off, and for some reason I resented it. I had accepted the fact that he was an unorthodox analyst, and I accepted Hans Bauman's statement that he was very good at what he did.

But this disconcerted me, which he was aware of.

"I don't ask people whether they're Jewish as a qualification for a relationship. Certainly, I have Jewish friends. Hans Bauman sent me to you."

"Yes. And didn't you mention something about your wife's great-grandfather on her mother's side who was some kind of a cabinet officer in the Confederacy during the Civil War?"

I sighed. "Yes, and what has that got to do with anything?"

"He was Jewish, wasn't he?"

"Yes. So I am told."

"And that would make her—what is it, one-eighth or is it one-sixteenth Jewish, if you go in for that kind of nonsense."

"I never gave it enough thought to try to work it out."

"Yet you brought it up," he insisted.

"What the hell do you want from me?" I snapped.

"I want you to talk about Buchenwald. Get angry. Get as angry as you have to."

"I'm not angry."

"Sure you're angry. Inside, you're burning. You want army talk? Fine. Just drop all this fuckin' shit, and forget that you're Scott Waring with all the walls you built around him, and talk! Talk about Buchenwald."

I stared at him as if I had never seen him before, and then I said wanly, almost like a child, "My time will be up."

It was pouring rain outside.

"You have all the time in the world, Scott. My next patient canceled."

"I don't know whether I can," I protested.

"Try. Sooner or later, you must."

"I don't know what I'll remember."

"Begin and you'll remember."

"Hans said we should do it. We could have passed by. Our unit wasn't part of the group that liberated it. We were on the Elbe. We took off in a jeep and we were there almost with the first troops—" My voice died away. I could only think of it in that manner. The part of me that was voice was dead. Of course I could speak, and in a whisper, I asked him for a glass of water.

"I have some Coca-Cola."

"No, just water, please." I drank the water, and then I asked him whether I could lie down.

"Sure."

He had one of those analyst couches in the room, leather, no arms, and a head rest at one end. I didn't want to look at him.

"They had the prisoners dig a mass grave. Before that, they just piled the bodies up outside. The prisoners told us—" I spoke slowly, repeating things. "The prisoners told us that before the guards knew it was over, they just piled up the bodies of the dead outside. They said that at one point there were more than a thousand bodies in the pile, starved, no flesh left on the bones, and the stench was unbearable, and then the weather turned—it was April, you know, and the stink became totally unbearable. We smelled the rotting flesh when we were still at least a mile away. God damn God, do you know the smell of rotting flesh?"

"I was a surgeon," Lieberman said harshly. "The kids' feet rotted in the foxholes."

"There was an open grave, maybe twice the size of this room. Filled with bodies. The bodies were skeletons covered with skin. There was a dead guard, an SS man, the top of his head had been shot away, and there was a prisoner in the pajamas they wore, and he was trying to hit the dead SS man with a spade, which he lifted so slowly, like slow motion, but he couldn't lift it high enough—God damn you, why do you want this?"

"Because I'm the doctor and you're the patient."

"They walked toward us, those who could, skeletons walking with the faces of skeletons, with the flesh gone and the skin stretched over the bones, and all I could think of was that they were dead but they didn't want to die, and the GIs near me were swearing and whimpering—you know, when I used to dream about it, I would become hysterical, but I was cold as ice."

"Before," Dr. Lieberman said, interrupting me, "you said God damn God."

"No."

"You didn't say it?"

"Why would I say something like that?"

"Why would you?"

"I don't know. I don't think I said it."

"Two months ago, when we first talked about Buchenwald, you said that one of the prisoners walked toward you. He had a shirt but no trousers, naked from the waist down. He had an erection. His mouth was wide open. Then he went down on his knees and rolled over. He was dead."

"I didn't tell you that."

Dr. Lieberman rose, went to his desk and returned with a notebook. He riffled through it. "Here it is," he said. "February 12th. The prisoner had an erection."

"How on God's earth," I asked him, "could anyone who had suffered through that, dying of starvation, yes, dying of starvation, have an erection?"

"It's possible. There's the center of a life force that makes the continuity of life possible. There's no force on earth greater than the drive of life to perpetuate itself. Never mind that. Why do you suppose you can't remember that you told me about that incident?"

"You say I told you."

"I'm not lying, Scott."

I closed my eyes and was silent and he was silent, and the minutes ticked away. Then I remembered. I told him that I remembered and I apologized for calling him a liar.

"You know, I'll dream about this again," I said bitterly.

"Perhaps not. Let's talk about the barracks."

"Why?"

"You mentioned the barracks. You said you never went into the barracks."

"I don't remember talking about the barracks. Why would I say I didn't go into the barracks?"

"I don't know. I asked you once about the barracks, and you said you didn't go into the barracks. The smell was too vile."

I sat up and faced him. Tears were coming down my cheeks. He handed me a box of tissues. I felt sometimes that I would have been more comfortable with a female therapist, who might on occasion offer a few shreds of sympathy. Sympathy was not Dr. Lieberman's cup of tea. He simply nodded and waited, and then he asked me, "What's that you're humming?"

I broke into laughter, tears and laughter; it was confusing for me to have to wonder whether I was laughing or weeping. "I was humming it," I said. "You said barracks. It's not that I simply lied to you. You keep taking me places I don't want to go. You say barracks, and I keep thinking about 'Lili Marlene.' That was when I was in North Africa, before they posted us to England for the invasion. Our battalion built a prison enclosure, very quick, neat, modern, Quonset huts, showers—we had about six hundred German prisoners, and every night they'd sit around and sing that wretched song, *Underneath the lamppost, at the barracks gate,* a very sentimental song—Germans are so fuckin' sentimental, and you say barracks, I dream of 'Lili Marlene,' don't I? You want me to talk about the barracks, I'll talk about the barracks. By the way, doc, permit a small discourse on the subject of shit—I mean you eat and it all turns to shit, doesn't it? George Bernard Shaw called us shit machines, as good a definition as any of the human race. Every day we fed a German prisoner a minimum of five thousand calories a day, frankfurters, potatoes, bread, fresh vegetables, you would not believe it."

"Let's get back to the barracks at Buchenwald," Lieberman said. "I want you to talk about it. The last time we tried, you said that Hans Bauman went in and you remained outside."

"No, I went in."

"All right. Now close your eyes. Go back there. Start at the door, go in. What did you see?"

I shuddered and let myself step through the gates of hell. This was my first venture into therapy, as they called it. My sister, Linda, brought it up. Linda was never one to allow a sense of delicacy to interfere with her right to help, as she saw help, where a member of her family was concerned. She also embraced that delight of some women, namely matchmaking. No one else would have had the presumption to tell me that I was obsessed with a woman long dead; and I suppose part of her lack of tact came from her efforts to find me a wife once I was lured back to the dinner table. She seated me next to several of the most attractive women she knew, in sequence of course, four in all, two divorced, two fresh out of college. When this failed to produce any evidence of normal lust on my part, she told me that she knew I was not queer—this was before the word gay came into usage—and that I was obsessed with Martha Pembroke, and that until I came down to earth and realized that Martha Pembroke was not the first and last woman on earth, I would go on allowing my life to slide by. I got angry and told her that it was none of her damn business, which elicited a very nice letter of apology on her part.

But her accusation stayed with me, and I brought the problem to Hans Bauman, who was not only a friend and my former commanding officer, but a father of sorts since my dad's death. There is a relationship with a commanding officer whom one respects and trusts that is unlike any other relationship except perhaps an athlete's feeling for his coach. Am I obsessed? I put it to him. I had avoided the psychology courses at MIT. I was suspicious and perhaps somewhat contemptuous of this meandering around in the human mind. Well enough for others, but nothing I needed, and the fact was that I knew practically nothing about psychiatry or psychoanalysis. When Hans Bauman told me that Max Lieberman was not a Freudian and that he had his own approach to treatment, he was signifying that I needed therapy.

Now, lured into the gates of hell, the doorway to the barracks at Buchenwald, I tried to hold back, angrily demanding of Dr. Lieberman, "This whole fuckin' thing is leading nowhere. Am I obsessed because I loved a woman? Am I the only man who ever loved like that? Am I sick because she is the central fact of my life?"

He smiled, a rare smile, and shook his head. "Scott, Scott— none of us ever used that word before the war. I don't mind it. I use it the same way—a sort of childish attention getter.

You want to leave, leave, but we are not going to talk about Martha—not today. You went into the barracks."

"I am not crazy," I said to him. "I can explain why I lied about going into the barracks—"

"I don't want to know why you lied or didn't lie."

"Well, there's something else you don't know, and I never could speak about it before." I left the couch and dropped into the chair where I usually sit. I had taken hold of myself. Something inside of me had snapped, loosened.

"Oh? Go on."

"I'm circumcised."

He nodded and shrugged. "Many Protestant babies are—in the good hospitals. It's not that unusual." He chuckled. "Interesting, isn't it, Scott, that with one foot in the doorway of that hellish barracks, you tell me you're circumcised? Of course, the Jews inside that barracks were circumcised. You probably have heard that years ago when a Christian child had to be circumcised, they'd call in a *mohel,* the Hebrew word for the fellow who did the circumcisions, and he'd mumble a prayer, and lo and behold, the child was Jewish—all nonsense, of course."

I did not like him at that moment, but he assured me that in the course of the therapy, there was no necessity that I should like him; and right now I felt a small twinge of pleasure at the fact that I could prick his irritating display of superiority.

"You don't understand," I said.

"No? What don't I understand? Tell me."

"I was circumcised in nineteen forty-seven. I was hardly a newborn infant. I was twenty-nine years old."

He had no rejoinder to that. He simply stared at me, and I let the silence stretch.

"You had an infection," he finally said. "That's not uncommon."

"No, I didn't have an infection. I was perfectly healthy. I just walked into Mt. Sinai Hospital up on Fifth Avenue, and I told them I wanted to be circumcised."

Dr. Lieberman nodded. "Well, I'll be damned. And they did it? Who operated on you?"

"The chief resident in surgery, I believe his name was Ackerman—or something of the sort."

It took a few minutes of silence for Dr. Lieberman to deal with this. I drank some water, and my brief moment of superiority floated away.

"You never told this—not to Hans, not to anyone?"

"No. It was my doing, my thing, my own damn penis, to be specific. Well, I told you."

"Because you're standing in the doorway of the barracks."

I told him. I closed my eyes and visualized it—and told Dr. Lieberman what I saw in my mind's eye. The barracks were long and narrow. On either side, all the length of the barracks were shelves, four of them between floor and ceiling, each shelf some fourteen inches from top to bottom and six feet in length. Envision a library where the bookshelves have uprights some six feet apart and the shelves are perhaps thirty inches deep. One steps out of the sunlight peering into the semi-darkness of the barracks, and one is greeted by the smell, a terrible smell, an awful smell. Of all the human senses, I am sure that the sense of smell is the oldest and deepest, the longest remembered, and this was the smell of rot and death and filth and feces and urine. In each of these shelves, one or two or sometimes three men were huddled, men of bones, every rib clearly evident, men whose faces had turned into skulls, men too weak and possibly too unbelieving to pull themselves out of the shelves and stumble into the fresh air. And the American soldiers who had gone into the barracks ahead of us, stood in horror and then ran past us to get outside and vomit.

And as I told him this, I saw tears on Dr. Lieberman's cheeks, and I took a sort of bitter pleasure in that, meanwhile pinning a medal on him, because I had made the trip again into something unspeakable.

"When you couldn't talk about it," he said to me, "was it there?"

"I'm not sure."

"I mean did you remember it? Was it something you remembered but could not put into words?"

"I don't know."

"Why did you tell me about the circumcision now? Can you put that together with the barracks, Scott? It's terribly important."

"I think I was just pissed off at you."

"Scott, you've been pissed off at me before."

"Yes, I suppose so."

"Your sister, Linda, what would her reaction be if you told her you went off and got yourself circumcised?"

"I think she'd have me committed. Is my time up?"

"I'll tell you when your time is up."

"Are you charging me for this extra hour?"

"You're damn right I am."

"Thank you."

"I think you realize that we've accomplished something important today. Now about Coburg—"

"I told you about Coburg."

"You said you went back there, that's all."

"Maybe that's all you have to know about it."

"Why don't you let me decide what I have to know and what I don't have to know. Isn't Coburg in the Russian sector?"

"Just outside of it, I believe. But the sectors were not defined then. All right. I drove back there. The house was still there. The girls were gone. She was there, alone."

"What was her name?"

"Berthe. She had a son, but the Nazis took him away to one of the camps. She never heard from him again. She lived there alone. The house had taken a shell upstairs but the roof was still intact. I brought food with me, enough food to last her a month. I didn't know whether she was alive or dead, but I brought the food just on the chance that she'd be alive, a case of Spam, a bag of potatoes, jam, canned fruit, frankfurters and half a dozen bottles of wine that we had appropriated along the way. Her own provisions consisted of some ersatz bread and a single piece of rotten sausage. She was an amazing woman, an absolutely amazing woman. She cooked up a wonderful meal, potatoes and frankfurters, and we finished off two bottles of Rhenish wine, and I guess we were both drunk." I stopped.

"Try to go on," he said gently.

"I went upstairs and I went to bed with her. Does that shock you?"

"For God's sake, why should it shock me?"

"Because it was the first woman I had gone to bed with since Martha died."

"The first—in five years?"

"That's right. She had a good body, a round, beautiful body, and she knew all there was to know about her business, and it was no good, no damn good at all. I was impotent."

"That's always a hard thing to face, Scott."

"I was relieved."

"Do you know why? You know, sometimes, drunk, it becomes impossible."

"It wasn't because I was drunk."

Then I was silent. I said nothing. He said nothing. The silence in the room became intense. He had a clock on his desk, the face toward him, turned that way, I suppose, so that a patient could not see it. Suddenly, the clock began to tick. Of course, it had been ticking all along, but I had not heard it. Now as if the silence had produced the sound, the ticking sound was plain and clear.

"If I go now," I said to him, "you charge me for the whole hour?"

"That's right."

"It's one hell of a way to earn a living!"

"You could look at it that way. Do you want to go now?"

"Fuck you!" I snapped. I always took off my wristwatch and put it in my pocket when the session began. He wanted it that way. He didn't want his patients checking the time. Now I took the watch out of my pocket and looked at it. "I have fifty minutes left. If I'm paying for it, I stay."

"Only forty minutes. It's a fifty-minute hour."

"Forty minutes then."

"Suppose we use it. I don't like to take money for nothing. When you were circumcised at the hospital, what did you tell them? I mean the doctor—what did you say his name was? Ackerman?"

"Ackerman."

"He must have asked you why," Lieberman said, his tone suddenly gentle.

When I made no reply to that, Lieberman, still speaking softly, said, "I mean, Scott, one just doesn't walk into a hospital and ask for an operation. The usual routine is for one's own physician, either on his own or with consultation of another physician, to decide on the need for the operation, and then to arrange for it at the hospital he's connected with. The first thing Dr. Ackerman or any other surgeon at Mt. Sinai would ask you is who your physician was, then he would consult with your physician."

"What in hell are you after?"

"Come on, Scott, let's stop playing games. Things happened to you that tore you to pieces. You don't come here to trade insults. You wake up screaming at night. You smoked enough pot to burn your lungs out. You tried to drown yourself in liquor—"

"I'm over that. I don't drink. I don't smoke pot."

"What happened last night?"

I surrendered. I began to cry.

He knew how I hated being brought to tears, and he said, "It's all right. It's good to cry. Let go of it."

"I was back in the barracks," I whispered. "It wasn't just a dream. I could smell it. You don't smell things in a dream. I was lying in one of the bunks, and I knew that unless I got out of there, I would die. But I couldn't. I couldn't move. I pleaded with my body to move, but I was too weak."

"Did you know you were dreaming?"

"Sometimes I know I'm dreaming. But last night—" He gave me a box of tissues. "I'm all right now," I said.

"You want some water?"

"No, I'm all right now."

Lieberman kept a thermos of coffee on his desk. He poured

a cup and handed it to me.

"Would it be better lying down?"

"No, I'd rather sit. I'm all right now."

"Shall we go on?"

"Yes. Sure, why not? My guts are hanging out."

"I want you to tell me about the circumcision. I want you to tell me what you told them at the hospital."

"What difference does that make?"

"Let me decide," Lieberman said quietly.

"OK. You're right. They didn't want any part of it at first. I spoke to another doctor at the hospital before I saw Ackerman, a Dr. Friedman. I manufactured a cock-and-bull story about parents who had been Jewish and turned Christian. I was really Jewish. I told him something about my experience in the war. I wanted to be a valid Jew."

"He bought that?"

"I think so. Anyway, he told me to think about it and come back the next day. I came back, and Friedman insisted on a physical, and then they did the operation. They insisted that I stay there overnight."

"Do you know why you did it?" Lieberman asked.

I shrugged and shook my head.

"Scott, what are you giving me?"

"Look," I said, "I'm not Jewish. I have no desire to be Jewish." I closed my eyes and shrunk into myself. "I thought it would end the impotence," I mumbled.

"I didn't hear that."

"I thought it would end the impotence!" I shouted.

"Yes."

I stared at him, angry now, naked now. In all the weeks I had been seeing him, I had never felt like this, naked, uncovered, filled with shame and self-disgust.

"But it didn't work," he said.

"No, damn you, it did not work!" I drank the coffee, cold by now. Lieberman offered to warm it, but I shook my head. I hated that cool, semi-detached look with which he observed me.

"Berthe," he said.

"I don't want to talk about Berthe."

"She saved your life. She didn't know you. There was no reason in the world for her to believe you, to put her life and her son's life in jeopardy, to feed you, to give you clothes, to give you money. My God, you tell a story about this woman like nothing I ever heard, and now you tell me you don't want to talk about her. Did you love her?"

"You're forgetting," I said, irritated. "I had seen my wife, the woman I loved and married, beaten—"

"Hold on!" he interrupted. "An hour ago, you told me you dreamed about Martha last night. Then you told me you dreamed about the barracks."

"I wasn't lying. I had that hideous dream about the barracks. Toward morning, I dozed off. I dreamed about Martha. Jesus, I don't know what the hell you're after, doctor."

"Just trying to earn my bread the hard way. I know it was

only hours since you saw Martha beaten that Berthe rescued you. But when you saw Berthe the second time, years later, it was more than hours since Martha died. You must have felt something for her."

"I felt gratitude."

"And that's why you went to bed with her? Out of gratitude?"

"She was old enough to be my mother."

"So she was old enough to be your mother. Is that how you see it?"

"Now we're onto the Oedipus shit."

"Scott, for weeks you lay there on that couch, spending your hard-earned money and my hard-earned time talking about your father and your grandfather and Martha, but you never said one word about your mother."

"You never asked me."

"I don't ask," Lieberman said.

"You don't ask? Today, you've done nothing but ask your lousy questions."

"That's right. Because today we've finally broken through. Because today we've hit pay dirt. I told you when we began that I'm not a Freudian. I do what I do, and sometimes I get lucky. I'll tell you something that's really nothing about impotence in a man your age, and it's nothing because sex is a dark alley through which we stumble more or less blindly. You were in love with a woman who was never real, who was never actually your wife—"

"She was the most real thing in my existence."

"We won't argue that. You're convinced that you murdered her, that if it weren't for your stupidity and that miserable gun your grandfather gave you, she would be alive today. Do you know that penance is self-inflicted punishment for sin? My God, you Christians are even more fucked up than us Jews. And then a woman did what your mother did and what Martha never did, she gave you life and sustenance and she gave you her body—and you can't say you loved her."

"The hell with you!" I cried. "I don't have to sit here and listen to that."

Lieberman spread his arms and said, "Of course you don't. I'm not a cop and this is no interrogation room. I don't perform miracles. All I can do is get you to look at yourself. You don't want that—go."

I stood up, and then I sat down. "I've got twenty minutes left," I said, glancing at my watch. "What do you mean, you struck pay dirt?"

"Talk about your mother."

"There's nothing to talk about. She's my mother."

"Tell me about her. What is she like?"

I was asking myself, Who is my mother? What is she made of? What goes on inside of her? Did I ever see her shed a tear for anyone, when my father died, when Martha was buried?

"I don't know what you want. My mother is my mother, a middle-aged widow."

"Beautiful?"

"I don't think of her that way. Yes, I suppose she's good-looking."

"Does she embrace you, kiss you?"

"For Christ's sake, Dr. Lieberman, I'm a grown man."

"So you are. Was Berthe your mother?"

"What kind of a stupid question is that?"

"The kind I usually ask. Why do you want to be Jewish? Haven't you enough pain?"

"I don't want to be Jewish. Can't we finish this right now?"

"You have fifteen minutes left," he reminded me. I thought of my mother at my father's grave. She was all in black. I remembered my sister saying how good my mother looked in black. When I was an adolescent, I had tried to picture my mother in bed with my father, both of them making love. Now I could remember having the thought, but I couldn't remember seeing them in bed together. I must have seen them in bed together when I was a child, but I couldn't remember that. They always had separate rooms.

"When you saw Berthe at the end of the war," Lieberman said, "her son was gone? I think you said that the Gestapo had killed him."

"That's right."

"And when you think of Berthe now, can you have an erection?"

How does the bastard know? I asked myself. That damn smile of his had melted all my resistance.

"Yes," I agreed.

"And you think of her often?"

"Yes."

"Pay dirt," Dr. Lieberman said, talking more to himself than to me. "Every day when I am through with my work, Scott, I say to myself, give it up. Go back to being a real doctor. You don't cure anyone, maybe you don't even help anyone. You're a unique patient, and our work together is different. You've helped me with a good many things I didn't understand, which is a strange confession for any shrink to make. So when I say, pay dirt, it's a sort of triumph on my part."

"Which means I'm more or less crazy than the others?"

"You're not crazy. It's sanity you suffer from. Don't give it up now. Come back tomorrow. I think we're almost there."

In my first session with Dr. Lieberman, I had said to him, "Suppose I lie?"

"It doesn't matter."

"I don't understand that. Why doesn't it matter?"

"We both have to learn. We both learn from the lies— maybe more sometimes than we learn from the truth."

I thought about that after I left his office on this day, and went back to my drawing board and pretended to work while my thoughts were everywhere except on my work. Mostly, I thought of that day, years before, when I drove a jeep down the same road I had traveled with the two SS men in 1939, the car loaded with food and wine, and a prayer that Berthe was still alive and that I could bring her my small gift. I didn't have too much hope. As smart as she was, she had played a dangerous game, and for her to have survived the years of the war would have been a miracle.

I was not sure I would recognize the house, but I did; there it stood, a wall shattered but the rest intact. I parked my jeep in front of the house and sat for a few minutes, staring at the house and allowing myself memories of that terrible night; and as I sat there, the door opened and Berthe came out. Five years is a long time, but she appeared to have changed very little. As with many plump women, her face was unwrinkled, but her hair had gone white. She walked down the front stairs, across the walk, tentatively, and said, in German, "Do you want something?"

Then she stared at me, moved closer.

"Do you remember me? I'm Scott Waring."

Her brow knit, she continued to stare, and then her face lit up. "God be praised," she whispered.

Still she held back.

"The American with the handcuffs. You saved my life."

Her eyes filled with tears. I got out of the jeep. She tried to smile. "You're so tall now." I hadn't grown. I was no taller than I had been five years before. She reached out to touch my blouse. "You're an officer."

"Yes—a major. I'm with the Engineers. My specialty is bridges."

"Oh, yes, that's so important."

"Well, not so important. Our army has thousands of majors."

She smiled at my poor joke, and said, "Shall we go inside? It's turning cold." When I began to unload the jeep, she asked, "What is all that?"

"A few things for you. I know how bad everything is. So many people are hungry."

She didn't refuse my gifts, and we carried the food and wine into the house. The memories of my few hours in the place struck me like palpable entities; my mind spun in time, almost a sort of vertigo. One forgets pain, but the memory of terror sticks. The kitchen, smaller than I remembered it, had that shabby look of a place long without repair. I seemed to recall shelves of food, jars of jam, boxes of cereal and crackers, cans of meat. The shelves were bare now. I watched her lay out the food on the counter, carefully, looking at each can, each loaf of bread, each box of cookies, and shaking her head over the ten-pound bag of frankfurters.

"Is your son here—Paul—that's his name, isn't it?"

"Yes. Paul."

"Is he with you?"

She shook her head. "No—the Gestapo took him away, in 1940. I pray he's still alive—in one of the camps. A few people are beginning to come back from the camps. It's strange. The Americans are not here yet and the Germans have gone. It's suddenly so terribly quiet. People stay in their houses. No one knows what will happen now."

I shrugged. "There's nothing to fear from us. Perhaps I can do something to help find Paul. Don't be afraid of our army."

For the first time she laughed. "Ah, sweet Herr Waring, what should I be afraid of? They have taken everything from me. I am the last Jew left in Coburg, and only because I had a whorehouse. They have a reverence for whorehouses, and why not? They have turned their whole country into a whorehouse. I listen to your radio—to the German language broadcasts—and I heard what they said about the concentration camps. Is it true?"

"Yes. I was there. I saw it."

"The radio said that they killed thousands and thousands of Jews, maybe millions, all the Jews in Germany, all the Jews in Poland. Can that be?"

"I don't know. I only saw one camp. It was terrible."

"Then we won't talk about that. Can you stay for dinner?"

"Of course. But you must call me Scott."

"All right. If you call me Berthe." She was sorting out the food. "What is Spam?"

"A kind of sausage meat. It isn't bad."

"I'll cook the frankfurters, with dumplings. And applesauce. Oh, I haven't seen applesauce for so long. And hot bread. Must you leave tonight?"

"I can stay overnight, if you have a place for me. I have two days of leave left."

"Then you will stay, and you will tell me everything that happened to you, and how you found your beautiful sweetheart Martha—" She paused, sensitive to my expression. "What happened?"

"Martha was dead. They beat her to death. We never spoke to each other again."

"Oh, God in heaven, what terrible things we've seen! I didn't know. A dozen times, Paul and I talked about you, but there was no way we could find out. We didn't dare to ask any questions, and no word of what had happened to the two SS men ever appeared in the Coburg paper. By mid-afternoon of the day you were here, a tow truck drove by the house, dragging the big Mercedes. But nothing else, no ambulance, no questions even, because just up the road are the stairs that lead down to the river." While she spoke, she stirred up the fire in the stove, put water up to boil, and mixed the ingredients for the dumplings. She poured a glass of wine for each of us.

"Poor boy, poor American boy, what a terrible thing to happen to you! What can I say? We are partners in sorrow."

She fussed over me, finding every possible way to comfort me for something that had happened five years before, while I thought of Martha's funeral, my mother standing beside me, dressed so stylishly in black that I heard people whisper, "Doesn't she look wonderful." And now here was this strange German woman, who had saved my life, who was Jewish, who spoke not a word of English, feeding me, mothering me, making me feel like a little boy lost who had come home at last. She was a good cook. She made a delicious dish out of frankfurters and dumplings, and she served it with hot bread and pickles and a mustard sauce, the bread being a biscuit of some sort; and we sat and drank wine and talked and talked about who I was and who she was, and she told me about her husband and her father and mother, and about going to the synagogue in Coburg when she was a little girl and seeing high on the wall the depiction in gold-plated metal of the two Lions of Judah braced against the tablets of the Law, the Ten Commandments, and how each time she said her prayers at night, she felt the protecting image of the two lions; and I spoke of my own earliest memories of a tiny white-shingled Congregationalist church in Connecticut that my father took me to one Sunday—my mother, whose family was Episcopalian, remained at home—and how I fell asleep during the sermon and thought I would be punished for that; and so each of us, wedded in the trust between one who has saved a life and the other whose life had been saved, spoke of things we had never spoken of to anyone, and became drunk, easily, slowly, and just as easily and naturally, we went upstairs to her bedroom and undressed and lay down in bed together.

It was the first time in the five years since Martha's death that I had been with a woman, and it was the first time that I had to face the fact that I could not consummate a sexual encounter; and she was so kind and so loving and so gentle that it did not matter a great deal, and I finally fell asleep pressed to her abundant soft bosom.

And now, twelve years had passed, and I sat at a drawing

board in an office in a skyscraper in New York City and brooded over whether I would go back to Dr. Lieberman the following day.

I did go back.

"You come here during your lunch hour, Scott," he said to me. "You have to manage to eat some lunch."

He was being nice, interested in something more than tearing my guts apart. This was a remarkable change.

"There's a hot dog cart in front of our building," I explained. "I have a frankfurter and eat it on the way over."

He made a face and informed me that good food was important. "Any dreams?" he asked.

"I didn't make notes, so I don't remember."

"Let's talk about your mother."

"All right," I agreed. "We'll talk about my mother."

If he was surprised, he didn't show it. He simply nodded, and we talked about my mother.

# II

When the bridge in Westchester County was completed, my job was over; but fortunately, just about that time, Holben-Chute decided to bid on bridge jobs, and took me in at a very nice wage, $10,000 a year, which at that time, in 1953, was very real money indeed. I was thirty-five years old, in good health, with a good job. I had finished my labors with Dr. Lieberman, and my head appeared to be screwed on reasonably well.

I had a small apartment on West 10th Street, the second floor in one of those lovely old red-brick townhouses, and in good weather, I welcomed the walk downtown to the financial center, where Holben-Chute had their main offices. My life was comparatively simple. Once a week, I dined with my mother, who was making the best of being a widow, uncomplaining and dedicated to the soup kitchen of her church. Once a month or so, my sister bullied me into a dinner party at her home or some charity affair. I went to the movies, read books at home while eating a sandwich and fruit and coffee, and two or three times a week I had dinner alone or with a friend at Jack's on 12th Street. I had sampled most of the Village restaurants, and had settled on Jack's as the most compatible. Now and then I invited a girl to have dinner with me, sometimes one of the small army of women who worked at Holben-Chute, and on a few occasions, women my mother found in her capacity as matchmaker. I never allowed things to turn to sex.

It was at Jack's that I met Janet Goldman. At many eating places, in midtown as well as in the Village, actors and actresses survived by waiting tables. After Janet had served me a couple of times, I sought out her table, and we became acquainted to the degree that people do in such circumstances. Then, one evening, she said, "There is absolutely nothing as lonely as a man sitting alone at one of these wretched tables, and the roast duck is wonderful tonight."

Janet was twenty-one at that time, a slender young woman, straight brown hair, which she wore banged and cut straight at shoulder length. She had brown eyes, a full mouth, small nose and chin. She was a good-looking woman but not strikingly so, not beautiful in the way I think of beautiful women. She was about five six in height. She had a slight, barely detectable foreign accent, and she always wore a long-sleeved black jersey top over a full skirt and on her feet, flats.

She was right about my state of mind. I was lonely, a little more so than usual, and I said, "When do you have dinner?"

She shrugged and said, "Later, if I'm hungry."

"Why wouldn't you be hungry?"

"You never waited tables," she replied.

"Look—" I groped for a title.

"Janet," she said.

"Janet. Suppose I skip the duck and have a sandwich and coffee, and then can I take you to dinner when you're through here? I mean, this is not just a pickup. I'm a regular customer, and that gives me some standing, doesn't it?"

"Absolutely."

"You're not married?"

"I'm not married. What's your name?"

"Scott Waring. I'm not married. I'm an engineer."

"Last week, you were with a very attractive girl."

I shrugged. "I try. We were not enthralled with each other."

She nodded. "It happens. You don't have to order a sandwich unless you can't wait until ten o'clock. We have a waiting line, and Jack suffers when he sees one person at a table for two. If you really want to take me to dinner, I'll meet you outside at ten o'clock. By then, all I dream about is sitting down, and if you want tired company, well, OK."

I went home, took a shower, and at ten o'clock, I was waiting in front of Jack's. At a few minutes after ten, Janet came out and made a slight bow.

"Where to?"

"La Choilette."

"Wow."

"It's all right. I'm rich."

At midnight, we were one of three couples still sitting in La Choilette, still talking, yet learning remarkably little about each other. She was Janet Goldman, born in Germany in 1932. She was a dancer. She had nine months of work in *Oklahoma!* That was her one big break. She had also done two shows on the road, and for the past two summers, she had worked in summer stock. Three times a week, she worked out with a group in a loft over Rappaport's Dairy Restaurant. She had no living relatives in New York or anywhere else in the United States. She loved Mozart, Debussy, Bach and jazz. She loved trumpet music. She had just finished reading *Catcher in the Rye,* and she didn't know what all the shouting was about. She lived in a one-room apartment on Minetta Lane, and she loved to walk up and down Fourth Avenue, prowling through the endless rows of book stands between 14th Street and 9th Street. "But I'm a totally ersatz intellectual, and I have a vast background of pure ignorance, and nothing in my life could compare with actually building a bridge. And you do build bridges."

"Well, not really," I explained. "Bridges are built by cities and states and counties, who let out the contracts to big construction firms. When I'm lucky, I'm let in on the planning and someone is willing to look at my plans and blueprints."

"But the bridge in Westchester—that was yours, didn't you say?"

"Yes, sort of. I showed them how they could save almost a

hundred thousand dollars, which is a lot on a small bridge. That does give you a foot in. That's how Ammann got the job of doing the George Washington Bridge, by proving out his theory of indeterminacy—" She shook her head. "We'll go there some time—and I'll show you."

"But all the bridges you built during the war—"

"Me and a thousand other guys. Pontoon bridges, mostly. They put me in a demolition team. Blowing up bridges."

"Still—you know, I listen to you and it's a wonderful profession. I suppose I'll simply go on dancing until I'm too creaky to move because, besides waiting tables, it's the only thing I can do properly."

Finally, even La Choilette decided it was time to close. She took my arm as we walked the few blocks to Minetta Lane. I noticed the way she moved, walked, a sort of easy undulating motion.

At the door to the building on Minetta Lane, she faced me and smiled, and said, "Do you know, Scott, you're very nice. Thank you for such a good evening."

I had a feeling that she did not want me to kiss her, or make any advance. I said goodnight, and she ran into the house. For someone who had just put in six hours of waiting tables, she was certainly alert and alive.

The following night, as I took my table at Jack's, I looked around for Janet Goldman. There was no sign of her, and my order was taken by a young man who looked like Paul Newman but perhaps not enough like Paul Newman. Jack stopped by, with that kind of stupid grin that manifests itself on such occasions.

"Nice girl," he said.

"I'm glad you noticed. Where is she?"

"You employ actors, you got to make allowances," Jack said. "They'd swim the Hudson River to get in on a call."

I had my dinner and went home and found myself sulking. I looked her up in the telephone book. A girl living alone puts her name in with only an initial, which is less a protection than a giveaway, and I picked up the telephone twice before I decided not to call her. In the morning, on my way to work, I crossed over to Second Avenue and stopped in front of Rappaport's Dairy Restaurant, gathered my courage—which was not first rate when it came to pursuing women—decided to enter, and then said to myself, The hell with it! I'm being a fool.

That night, I had a corned beef sandwich and a bottle of beer in my apartment. I read the newspaper and then listened to some music on the radio, and at eleven o'clock, I called her number and immediately apologized.

"That's all right," she said. "I never go to bed before midnight. I'm glad you called. I missed you tonight."

"Dinner at my mother's," I lied, explaining awkwardly, "she's a widow—you know—"

"Of course."

"Do you think—tomorrow night, well, it's Saturday. Do you work tomorrow?"

"It's the big night. I'm on until eleven-thirty, and by then I'm absolutely dead."

"Oh. Yes, I can understand that."

"Sunday?" she said. "I'm off Sunday. We could have brunch, say about noon, and then we could go up to the park or down to the Battery or something. April is a wonderful month if you're lucky. Did you look at the weather?"

"Fair and sunny."

"Front of my house—twelve noon, right?"

"I'll be there."

I must admit that I could not wait for Saturday to be over and for Sunday to take its rightful place on the calendar. I walked. I went to the movies and watched a British film about the British fleet versus the German fleet in the war. I restrained my impulse to have dinner at Jack's, and thereby to see Janet Goldman. That would be too tacky, I decided; and I argued myself into facing the fact that I was not in love with her. I had been in love once in my life, and it was the kind of love that people dream of and write songs and poems about, to the ecstasy and the glory of the feeling. I knew what it was to be in love. I had never known that feeling with another woman, and certainly I did not feel it with Janet Goldman. I liked her. I liked her company. That was it.

But that was hardly the whole truth. I had spent one evening with her, a good, comfortable, easy evening, and I missed her. And above all, I was not lonely with her and I was not sorry for myself.

Sunday, at twelve noon, I stood in Minetta Lane waiting, and almost on the minute she came downstairs and there she was, with me wondering why this ritual of meeting her downstairs, and certainly I would not be put off by her apartment, and surely she knew that. She wore a knit yellow shirt, tight to her body, revealing a supple form and small breasts, the body of a dancer, and a loose black skirt, black stockings and flat shoes. She carried a cardigan sweater, also black. She looked good.

"Put on the sweater," I suggested. "It's chilly."

"Oh, no, it's not chilly, it's delicious." She held out a hand in greeting, no more to kiss me, nor did I try to kiss her. "What wonderful place do we go for brunch?"

"Now I have a reputation to live up to," I said. "We're going to the Edwardian Room in the Plaza. Do you like it?"

"I've never been there. Can we walk? The Edwardian Room." She shook her head and grinned.

"We'll walk later."

We took a cab. I asked her about the call. "Did you get the part?"

"Oh, no, it wasn't that kind of thing. I spent Friday at Saks Fifth Avenue. I wore a little ruffled pink skirt, and I sprayed perfume on ladies who wanted perfume sprayed on them, and then I pointed them to the counter where it was sold. There were four of us."

"Why?" I wondered.

"Why? Scott, I got forty dollars for eight hours of spraying

perfume—a lot easier and more profitable than waiting tables. Anyway, my agent got it for me, and I couldn't say no
to her. I told Jack it was a call. He's good about that kind of
thing. And it was fun. I don't get to Saks very often." She
looked at me curiously. "You don't understand, do you? They
have to have union people."

"What makes you think I don't understand?"

"Well, perhaps you do. Anyway, I have never been to the
Edwardian Room. I went to the Plaza once—with some of the
kids. But the prices! You're very rich, aren't you?"

"Absolutely. I make ten thousand a year."

"Wow!"

"Oh, come on. That's not so much. You did have that long
run in *Oklahoma!*"

"Yes. I was lucky—maybe the last time ever."

She was totally ingenuous. She had no tricks of enticement
or flirtation. I had the feeling that she was absolutely pleased
to be with me, but not in the sense of coming on to me.
There was no pretense. She was delighted with the menu at
the restaurant, and she ordered a proper meal, sausage and
eggs Benedict, and an enormous baked apple to begin and a
Floating Island for dessert, offering as an apology only the
fact that she never gained weight. "In fact," she said, "when I
do work and start dancing, I lose weight and I can't eat
enough to keep my weight up."

"What do you weigh?"

She burst out laughing. "Oh, Scott, I never knew anyone who

asked me what I weigh. Anyway, I never went out with anyone like you—an engineer who builds bridges."

"Who do you date? And don't tell me that anyone as good-looking as you doesn't date."

"I date sometimes," she admitted. "Mostly with kids who are dancers. They—"

She broke off and spooned out gobs of the Floating Island and filled her mouth with it, leaving me to wonder whether she was going to tell me that she dated gay people who didn't make passes at her. Anyway, she changed the subject and asked me what I'd like to do with the afternoon.

"Whatever you want to do."

"Do you know what I want to do? I want to go uptown to the George Washington Bridge, and I want you to show me what a brilliant and wonderful thing that engineer—what's his name?"

"Ammann."

"—yes, what he did that no one else ever thought of doing, that indeterminacy thing?"

"Really? Why?"

"Because I like you, and I don't know anything much about anything, including bridges, except dancing."

"There's an Australian group at Carnegie Hall, and they're doing *Swan Lake*. It's practically across the street from here, and I thought we'd walk over and get tickets—"

"Did you reserve the tickets?"

"No, we can buy them at the box office."

"Now? Never. They'd be sold out, and anyway I've seen *Swan Lake* three times, and that's enough. I'd much rather do the bridge if you don't mind? And if you want to see dance, some friends of mine are in *Billy the Kid,* next Sunday, at the Brooklyn Academy, and we can see that—unless next Sunday is taken and you have enough of me today?"

"I don't have enough of you. Not yet," I assured her.

"Am I very pushy?"

"I don't think so. We'll go up to the Cloisters, and we'll find a place there where there's a good view of the bridge, and I'll be delighted to lecture on the bridge. And if that gets too boring, we'll walk around the Cloisters."

She was as pleased as if I'd given her something priceless. She had never been to the Cloisters. In fact, New York above 59th Street was mostly unknown territory for her. She had been to the Metropolitan Museum once, but her world stretched from the Village to the theatre district, and not much more than that.

We rode uptown in a cab, with Janet watching the meter suspiciously, and the Cloisters, standing in a sea of spring blossoms high on the ridge overlooking the Hudson River, made her gasp with delight. We found a section of the stone balustrade where the bridge was clearly visible, and I fell into my own enthusiasm. "It's absolutely wonderful," I told her, "one of the greatest achievements in mankind's whole history of construction. If there were a poetry of technical things, this would be a celebratory sonnet. People don't realize that.

They simply take it for granted."

"I would have," she confessed. "I did a summer in a little theatre in the Ramapos, and we drove across and I never thought twice about it."

"Absolutely, and why not? But look at the weight in the middle, with the stream of cars flowing across it. Why doesn't it just pull out of the ground? The maximum pull of each cable is sixty-two million pounds, and the cables alone, without the roadway, weigh millions of pounds. Those four steel cables—each of them woven with almost twenty-seven thousand parallel steel wires—support the roadway and its traffic over a distance never bridged before with a single span. Yes, the Golden Gate Bridge is longer, but this was the first, and those towers are twice the height of the Palisades across the river. The whole bridge is simply a miracle."

"Yes, I see what you mean."

"I watched it being built when I was a kid. That's one of the things that made me want to be an engineer and build bridges."

"Tell me what that man Ammann did."

"He did the impossible. Someone always does the impossible, and then it works, and people say, of course. Now, look at the tops of the towers. There are two cables on each side—perhaps you can make out the big rollers they rest on. Each pair of cables is positioned on the inside edge of the towers. You see that?"

"Yes. Is that strange?"

"Also wrong, by every stricture of engineering. It was a

given of engineering lore that cables must rest on the centers of the towers, since that was the point of greatest strength. But if they were hung from the center of the towers, the deck of the bridge would have to extend to the center of each tower, and since cars couldn't drive through the towers, that part of the deck that overlapped the towers would be useless, even though it cost millions of dollars to build. But every design except Ammann's had the deck hung from the center of the towers. Do you follow me?"

"So far, yes."

"Ammann hung the deck from the inside of the towers, which meant that his costs were millions of dollars less than any other designer's, and every engineer who looked at his plans hooted them away and stated flatly that the bridge Ammann designed would fall down. The cables had to be hung from the center of the towers."

Oh, I admit that all of this was to impress her, and that it was sort of childish of me to want so much to impress her and make her think that I was Mr. Wonderful because I knew about the bridge and had studied at MIT; but I was taken with her more than I understood or could admit at the time.

"But they're not," she said, "and why doesn't the bridge fall down?"

"All right. Notice how the towers are braced with the steel beams. Ammann said that the weight on the inside of the tower would cause it to collapse, but as the collapse began, the crisscross of beams would take and redistribute the weight right back to its point of origin. Thereby, the collapse of the tower would never take place."

She smiled hopelessly. "Now you lost me."

"I think he lost every engineer who looked at his plans. The plain fact of the matter is that the bridge is eternally falling but never falling, which is the indeterminacy thing I told you about."

"Then how did he ever get it built?"

"By taking all the money he had and building a scale model. They tested his model in every possible way—and it worked." I had to confess that I did not understand it completely either, but I was to call it to mind later, as you will see.

When I suggested that we might amble through the Cloisters, she shook her head and shivered slightly.

"You're cold."

"No, I'm not cold. Scott, what are your plans for tonight?"

"I thought we might spend the whole day together, but I guess I've bored you to tears."

"Oh, no. No, it was fascinating. I'm stupid about such things and I feel ashamed, I want so much to understand."

"So do I."

"You're being sweet."

"Sweet. I feel like a pedantic idiot."

It was turning quite cold, and it was just past four o'clock. I suggested that we go back downtown, and she could pick up a coat at her place, and that I would get my coat and a bottle of champagne from my fridge, and then stop by for her, and we'd have the champagne and then go out to dinner.

"Scott, you'll be so tired of me by then."

"Let me decide when I'm tired of you."

"Then I'll meet you at your place. Mine is a mess. The truth is, I didn't get out of bed until eleven."

"As you wish."

I dropped her off at Minetta Lane. "In about an hour?"

"Scott, I don't have your address."

I gave her the address, and then I walked home. I felt good, better than I had felt in years. I had found someone I liked, someone I could talk to, someone who did not make me uneasy or fill me with guilt. I wondered whether I was pressing it too hard. A whole day? I had never felt either clever or more than very ordinarily decent looking. Yet I was quite sure that she liked me.

I had left my bed unmade, and I straightened it now. It was a decent apartment, one very large room at the front of the house, a smaller bedroom behind it, and a tiny kitchen. I had furnished it myself to my own taste, two big couches flanking a fireplace, some easy chairs, and a big old chest that I picked up at a second-hand furniture place. A big rug with a modern design. The house, I was told, dated from 1820, and had been refurbished. The fireplace still worked and I quickly stuffed paper under three of the synthetic logs that I bought at the local supermarket. By the time she rang the downstairs bell, the fire was burning briskly.

She had changed her skirt, and now she wore a loose printed thing. She came into the room slowly, tentatively; she looked around and smiled. "What a beautiful room!"

I told her to sit down and warm herself at the fire, and I took her jacket, and then I went into the kitchen, opened the bottle of champagne that was in the fridge, and returned to the living room with the bottle and a couple of glasses. Janet stood in front of the chest, staring at two photos that were on the chest in Plexiglas frames. One was a wedding picture, Martha and I, and the other was an eight by ten photo of Martha.

"What a beautiful woman!" Janet said. Then she turned to me, her dark eyes questioning.

"That's Martha, my wife."

"You said you weren't married."

"Martha died in nineteen thirty-nine."

"Oh, I'm sorry." She stared at the picture again. "She's so beautiful—and so young." She turned to me and shook her head and put her hands up to her face.

"I should have told you."

"No. It's not my business. Nineteen thirty-nine. That was fourteen years ago. You never married again."

"No."

"You must have loved her very much."

"Yes, I did."

"We became such good friends," she said forlornly. "We are good friends, aren't we, Scott?"

"Very good friends."

"I haven't asked you how your wife died."

"Last week was important. Today was important."

"And the past, Scott, isn't that important? Why didn't you tell me?"

"I didn't know how," I said lamely. "It's not a story I can tell easily."

"You were very young."

"Yes, I was still in college. So was she. We were in love and we were married, and went to Europe—to Germany. Martha was murdered by the Gestapo."

For a long moment, she simply stared at me, her lips parted; then, in words that were a whimper of agony, she whispered, "Oh, my God, how terrible." Her eyes filled with tears. I went to comfort her, but she drew away. Then, suddenly she pulled her long-sleeved jersey top over her head, leaving her body naked to the waist except for her brassiere, and held out her right arm, on which were tattooed a set of numbers. "Look at it," she whispered. "I am always afraid to show it to anyone. I didn't want to show it to you. I felt that if I showed it to you—that would be the end, yes? But you know. Other people don't know. It won't be the end, will it, Scott? Oh, I want so much for it not to be the end."

"No, it won't be the end." I took her in my arms and kissed her and tried to hold her close. But she pulled away from me, suddenly and with violence, thrusting my arms aside, literally wrenching herself loose. She reminded me of a wild animal, trapped, and the image persisted as she retreated across the room, her eyes wide and staring.

"Don't you see?" she cried, almost in a scream. "Don't you see? Don't you understand?" She pointed to the numbers tattooed on her arm. "You can't!"

"Janet, what did I do?"

"I'm not a person. I'm not someone you can love. I only want you to be my friend. My God, I'm not a woman. I thought you'd understand when you told me about her." She pointed to the picture of Martha.

"You're frightened. What did I do?" I walked toward her, and she backed away. "Janet, please, don't be afraid of me. Look, I'll stand here. I won't move. Don't you see that I care for you? I don't know what to say."

She seemed to relax a bit. "You can't love me. No one can love me. I'm not a woman."

"You're a wonderful, beautiful woman."

She was struggling with her jersey, and as she pulled it over her head and thrust her arms into the sleeves, I retreated as far as I could, seating myself across the room from her. "It's all right, Janet," I said gently. "It's all right."

She picked up her jacket.

"Please don't go, Janet."

She stood with the jacket in her hand, looking at me as if she had never seen me, and again I had the impression of a trapped animal. And then, as if whatever had taken hold of her passed as quickly as it came, she let go of the jacket and dropped onto the couch, dissolving into tears, her face covered by her two hands.

I said nothing and waited. And then, speaking in German, she whimpered, "Oh, God help me, what a fool I make of myself."

"Oh, no," I said softly in German, "we are not fools. We walked through hell, both of us. Does that make us fools?"

She uncovered her face, and regarded me questioningly, wiping the tears with her hands.

"I speak German, Janet. Is it easier in German?"

She shook her head.

"Please talk to me," I said, in English now.

"I can't."

Then I went over to her and knelt in front of her, taking her hands in mine. "Never be afraid of me."

She nodded.

"I love you."

"How? How?"

"With all my heart."

"I have to tell you—"

"No, not now." I got up then, drew her to her feet, and when I took her in my arms, she seemed to melt.

"I can't love," she whispered. "It was taken away."

"We'll see. We'll try."

"I'm afraid."

"So am I," I said. "I'm terribly afraid. But we'll try."

# III

We made love, passionately, deeply—both of us starved, as if we had both been dead and found life in each other, and my impotence vanished in a kind of delight and agony, and we talked and wept and dried our tears and made love again. This was the first time I had slept with a woman—barring my failed attempt at Coburg—since Martha's death, and it was Janet's first intercourse with a man since she had been raped by a guard at Dachau at age eleven, and kept alive by him and repeatedly beaten and raped during the next nine months before liberation.

We poured out our pasts to each other, and made love and talked and talked, and made love again, and lay naked side-by-side, and touched each other and caressed each other and marveled that we had found each other. I looked at her slender, lovely body, and tried to comprehend what a woman was who could go through what she had gone through and remain so gentle and innocent of hate. We wept because the things we told each other could not be told without tears. Her father had been a physician in Munich, her mother a school teacher, and they had lived in Munich for as many generations back as could be traced, but they were Jews and because they were Jews, they had been destroyed, her mother, father, two sisters and a brother, aunts, uncles, cousins, every shred of family that she knew of—all into the gas ovens and the execution pits. Only she had survived through a guard's lust for a skinny eleven-year-old child.

There was a moment, as we talked and made love that Sunday night, when Janet lapsed into German once again, a child's German, but when I replied in the same language, she gritted her teeth and shook it off angrily. She had spoken no German since leaving Europe. After liberation, she had lived for a time in a Quaker hospice in France, and then she had been brought to America by the Jewish Federation. For three years, she had lived in a Jewish institution for war orphans, sternly unwilling to be put out for adoption. "I loved my father and mother too much," she told me. As a child in Munich, she had been given lessons in ballet from age six. When she was sixteen, she found a job in one of a chain of Jewish-owned candy shops. Once she came to America, until this day, she never again spoke German. She had a good ear, and she picked up the language quickly. "I had to rid myself of everything German," she said. "But I still have a little accent, don't I?" But it was less an accent than a formality of speech that I found as endearing as everything else about her.

By midnight of that Sunday, we had poured out our hearts to each other. We were limp, exhausted and hungry. We dressed and wandered through the Village streets until we found a bar on 8th Street where they served food. We stuffed ourselves with hamburgers and fried potatoes, and then we went back to my apartment and made love again and slept in each other's arms until eleven on Monday morning. I called my office and pleaded a cold. She went to Jack's where her stint began at two o'clock, and until ten, when I would pick her up, I wandered through the streets of the city, marveling at how wonderful everything I saw had become, and at the fact that everything looked different.

So began a period of some seven weeks that Janet and I were together. I would go to the rehearsal hall over Rappaport's when she had her practice class, usually between eight and nine in the morning, before the regular shows turned up for rehearsal, and then we would have breakfast downstairs at that marvelous restaurant—soon to be closed and gone forever—facing each other across a mountain of dry rolls, sour rolls, sweet rolls, bagels and that delicious concoction of flour and onions called a Bialy, and then she would walk with me downtown to the financial district, where I was excused for my lateness by working an hour or two overtime in the evening.

For three of the seven weeks, Janet rehearsed—at the same loft over Rappaport's—for a perfectly awful off-Broadway musical, which closed after a week. Including rehearsals, I saw the show at least six times and came away with a selection of unsingable songs. Jack, whom I began to understand as a patron of out-of-work actors, willingly took Janet back. On and off, he rescued at least two dozen unemployed youthful thespians and dancers, and when there was no work, he fed them. Sundays, we spent together. I found myself enjoying *Billy the Kid* and admired Martha Graham's troupe, and managed never to let Janet know that a good deal of dance bored me. Hers was a world I had never known, and I must confess that if dance was not my favorite form of expression, I learned a good deal about the art and came to appreciate it.

We were well attuned to each other, and if this was not the same youthful, romantic passion I had experienced with Martha, it was still something that filled a great need in my life. We never spoke of marriage. It was in my mind, and possibly it was equally a part of her thoughts; and certainly, the more I saw of Janet, the more empty my years after the war became. The thought of returning to the meaningless life I had led in the years before I met her chilled my blood. The decision to have her meet my mother was inevitable. I had been neglectful of my mother, who never missed an opportunity to tell me that it was time I thought of marriage and a family, and who, as I mentioned, had manipulated me into dates with this or that young lady whom she thought might make a proper wife, according to her standards. My mother had just passed her fifty-seventh birthday, still an attractive woman, still living alone in the same East Side apartment she had shared with my father. She was an honorary member of the board of directors of Waring Aeronautics, a very large company now and one of the leaders in the manufacture of fighting planes—a company in which she held a large stockholder's interest. Although my father had taken great pains to understand my philosophical position and came to accept my hatred of war and the service, and therefore never pressed me to join him in his business, my mother brushed my feelings away as a youthful bit of idealism. I suppose that in the years after my father's death—he died while I was in the service—she felt that my distaste for the company and my refusal to have any part of it or accept any of the stock she offered me was a sort of betrayal. It was a subject we both avoided sedulously.

Now, after seven weeks of my relationship with Janet Goldman, she called and scolded me for avoiding her.

"I'm sorry. Suppose I come to dinner?"

"You see, you can be nice to a poor old widow."

"Mother, you're not poor and you're not old. Would this coming Sunday be all right?"

"Why on Sunday? I met a delightful young woman and we spoke about you. She's divorced—but please don't think of that in a negative manner. She's twenty-seven and she married some ridiculous European count or something—I think he was Hungarian, I mean before the communists took over—and I am not arranging anything, but she is someone you should meet. She goes off on Saturday, her folks have a place in the Hamptons. Well, her mother is an old friend. So if you come Friday night?"

"Mother, I want to bring a girl for you to meet."

"Really!"

"Really. Yes, Mother. And Sunday is the only night we can make it. Are you free for Sunday?"

"I will make myself free. Who is she? Is this serious, Scott? Please tell me that it's serious."

"Mother, I simply want you to meet her."

"What is her name?"

"Janet. Eight o'clock—yes. Or is that too late?"

"Eight o'clock."

But when I told Janet, she shook her head. "No. No, please, Scott. I don't want to."

"Why?"

"Because from all you told me about your family, I know that this makes no sense."

"Darling, you'll have to meet her sooner or later."

"Why? Why will I ever have to meet her?"

"Because I intend to marry you. Hasn't that ever occurred to you?"

"It has occurred to me," she said slowly. "You never mentioned it before."

"I'm mentioning it now."

"Scott, I'm Jewish."

"I was aware of that."

"I have no family. I have no one. I was raped. Do you know

how many times I was raped? I don't know whether I could ever have a child. Who am I?"

"You're someone I love."

"And still you cling to Martha. Every time I go to your place, it's there, staring me in the face."

"It's a picture. Must I forget Martha to love you?"

"Oh, Scott, look at me," she said woefully. "I'm a Jewish girl with a number tattooed on my arm. That's all I am. I'm Jewish. I look Jewish."

"No one looks Jewish!" I shouted. "That's bullshit and you know it's bullshit! You're a beautiful young woman—"

I had never shouted at her before, never raised my voice to her. She began to cry, and I took her in my arms. She whispered, "I'll go, Scott. If you want me to, I'll go."

"You don't have to."

"I do. If I want to be with you, I do. You don't have to marry me, Scott."

"That's up to me—and to you. If you don't want me?"

"Scott! Oh, you don't know how I want you."

"No more tears. It breaks my heart when I see you cry."

"No more tears."

"And about being Jewish, Martha's great-grandfather was Jewish. He was some kind of cabinet official in the Confederacy—you know, the government of the South during the Civil War."

"Scott, I don't believe you. You're saying that to make me feel better. Suppose she hates me?"

"No one could hate you."

Sunday evening, at seven o'clock, I called for Janet at her apartment. The apartment consisted of a single room, twelve by eighteen, and a tiny alcove kitchen, and its decoration underlined the simple good taste she displayed in her manner, her clothes, and in the things she loved. Her bed was queen-sized with a hand-woven white spread, and piled with pastel-colored pillows. Two of the walls were painted white, the other two lemon yellow. There were two overstuffed chairs, upholstered in chintz printed with flowers. There were two area rugs, Portuguese needlepoint. On the walls, there were two large, framed prints, one of Isadora Duncan and the other of Martha Graham. When she let me in, she was wearing a simple, long-sleeved dress, printed silk.

"Is it all right?" she wanted to know. "Is it too dressy? I changed three times. Oh, I wish I could wear high heels, Scott, but I can't. I just wobble all over the place. These are my best Ferragamo. Are they all right?"

"You look beautiful. The shoes are fine."

"Shall I wear makeup? I mean, I have a little eye shadow, but no rouge. I never wear lipstick, I don't know how. Except on the stage, so I have some. It's makeup lipstick, and when I wear it, I feel foolish. But if I don't wear it, will your mother think I'm some sort of feminist?"

"You are, aren't you?"

"No, not really."

"Then don't wear it. You don't need it."

"Scott, what shall I talk about? I want her to think—I mean I want to make a proper impression."

Laughing, I took her in my arms. "You absolutely will make a most proper impression. My mother is a very nice lady, who suffers from coming from a fancy Southern family, which doesn't amount to beans here in New York. We'll roll right over her and you'll snow her completely." All of which was bitter proof that I knew my mother very little indeed.

On the other hand, Janet admitted defeat before the contest even started, if it could have been called a contest. My mother's apartment—the same apartment we had lived in when my father was alive—was part of a huge white-stone-faced building on 72nd Street between Fifth and Madison Avenues. It is part of the arrogance of coming from a well-to-do home that one accepts it as the normal course of things, and it had not occurred to me that Janet had never set foot in a place like this before. The doorman who opened the door of our cab greeted me comfortably, no stranger myself, but Janet faced a lioness's den. The enormous, high-ceilinged lobby, dating from the nineteen-twenties, when the apartment house had been built, set her aback again, albeit she tried not to be overwhelmed. I squeezed her arm reassuringly. The elevator operator, Anthony by name, observed that it was a long time since my last visit, once again raising the wall between herself and this strange, closed corporation of wealth that her lover, Scott, was a part of. I had not thought to tell her that this apartment was, by my standards, ridiculous, three bedrooms, my father's study, living room, dining room, library, and three servants' rooms behind the kitchen—and now occupied by one wealthy woman who was my mother; and now it was too late. I was in despair for my insensitivity, and I determined to set it right later, after we left.

I suppose you have to write something down, and think of how to put it, and think about it and brood over it to understand it properly. The plain truth of the matter is that I must have known what would happen. Afterwards, Dr. Lieberman suggested as much to me, that I was not bringing Janet to my mother for her to meet my mother, but to measure her against Martha. An obsession is a strange, dark thing. In the living room of my mother's house, there was a fine old Steinway piano. My mother played the piano, but not very much since my father's death, and the cover was down, never tilted in my memory since he passed away, and on the piano were half a dozen pictures of Martha and myself. Certainly, I had seen the pictures sitting there on the piano perhaps twenty, thirty or a hundred times. Afterwards, I thought that I could have arranged the meeting in a restaurant—or could I have done so? Or said to my mother, put them away, in a drawer or anywhere. That might have made no difference. Or I could have said, I am bringing Janet to meet you, just you, not Linda, not her damn husband, John Farraday. My justification was that I had not dreamed that she would invite them, but then as Dr. Lieberman pointed out, I knew very little of my mother.

They were all there when we arrived, and like me, Janet had expected only my mother. My mother is a tall woman, five feet and nine inches, and Linda had inherited her height. Farraday was a caricature of a banker, six feet and one inch, groomed grey hair, clean meaningless features, and my sister, Linda, appeared in a thousand dollars' worth of designer dress.

"This is my " My what? My dear friend? My love? My bed and Sunday companion? "Try to look at yourself," Lieberman had said to me again and again. "How would you describe yourself?" As a confused shit, was the essence of my reply.

"This is Janet," I said. "This is my mother. My sister, Linda. John Farraday."

My mother nodded. I have heard her described as regal, the result of a proper combination of snobbery and genetics. Tonight was the first time that it occurred to me that I did not like her very much.

"How nice to meet you at last," Linda said, implying long discussions with her about Janet. The fact was that I had only mentioned her once in a telephone conversation.

Farraday said hello with a slight smile, reserved for the female of the species, whatever you are, you're a cute number.

Janet stood up to the ordeal. She nodded and smiled. It was a dinner for only five, but my mother had hired a maid and bartender-butler to supplement her cook and housekeeper. We had drinks in my father's study, which my mother had refurbished. The only trace of my father that remained, aside from a picture of him on a black enameled chest of drawers, was a small model of the fighting plane he had designed at the onset of World War Two. Janet took a glass of white wine. The rest of us had martinis. I felt that I needed a drink.

"How nice to have you here," Mother said. "Have you known Scott a long time?" she wanted to know, explaining that I was not a confiding type.

"A few months," Janet replied.

"You've done wonders with this room," Linda said. My mother had done the redecorating at least five years ago, but Linda was feeling her way. Farraday put in that I was a lone wolf type.

"I never thought of Scott as a lone wolf," Janet said.

"Like all long-married men," Linda said, "John envies any man who reaches his thirties unmarried. It's the seven-year itch."

"Where do you live, my dear?" Mother asked.

"I have an apartment on Minetta Lane."

"Minetta Lane?"

"A small street in the Village," I told them.

"That's the wonderful thing about New York," Mother said. "You think you know the city, but you never do, really."

"I suppose not," Janet agreed. "Especially in the Village and down in the financial district. Scott took me to the Cloisters. I never saw it before."

"Never been there," John Farraday said.

"Thomas Wolfe said that no man knows Brooklyn—or

could," from Linda, who asked her husband, "Have we ever been there, John?"

"Of course we have. Frank Daley at the bank lives there, on Brooklyn Heights. We've been to his home."

"That's not Brooklyn."

"I know less of Brooklyn that I do of France," I admitted. "But Janet took me there. We went to see *Billy the Kid.*" I was feeling my way, and already I felt that I was treading on glass.

"*Billy the Kid?*" Mother wondered.

"Modern dance," Linda explained.

"Of course, Scott said you were a dancer."

"Ballet?" Farraday asked.

"I was trained for ballet, but mostly it's modern dance— when I can get work, or in a musical if I am lucky, or anywhere else where there's a call for dancers."

"How interesting," Mother said.

"Scott and the dance," Linda said. "I can't imagine Scott at a dance recital."

The direction was wrong, the tone was wrong, everything was wrong.

"It's so long since I had both my children here for dinner," Mother said.

"Then Janet has worked a small miracle," Linda said. "Do you live alone, my dear?"

"We don't live together, Linda," I told her.

"That was not what I meant."

"I don't have a roommate, which is what Linda meant, Scott. I have a tiny apartment, much too small to share." Janet was not floundering. I could see that she was desperately trying to take the measure of my family, relate me to it, relate me to the huge apartment, and put it all in focus for herself. Somehow, I was learning a great deal about her. I had missed the streak of iron that had allowed her to survive. "And I am very lucky," she added. "I pay thirty-five dollars of rent a month. If you're in the theater, the natural scheme of things is being unemployed."

"Doesn't your family help you at all?" Mother wanted to know.

"I have no family, no mother, no father, no sisters, no brothers, no uncles, no aunts."

A sheet of silence descended, and I tried to struggle through it. "Janet's family," I said, "was murdered by the Nazis. She is the only one who survived."

She came into focus for them now, perhaps for the first time. They had seen her but not looked at her; now they looked at her. I'm not sure they heard her accent; she was very good at covering it when she paid attention to it. "How awful!" Linda exclaimed. "I'm so sorry, so very sorry."

"Damned awful," Farraday muttered.

"Then you're German," Mother said.

"No, Mrs. Waring, I am not German. I am Jewish."

I was not too inventive. "I'm starved," I said.

"I think Mother means that you were born in Germany," Farraday said.

"Yes, I was born in Germany."

"I think dinner's ready, Scott," Mother informed me. "Would you take Janet into the dining room?" She rose and stood, very stiff, chin up, head raised; and like that, with the careful makeup she had put on for this evening when her son, Scott, was bringing a woman to her home, and with the facelift she had undergone two years before, she was indeed a beautiful woman. Without words, this beautiful woman of fifty-seven years spoke to the dancer with the dark bangs and the cheap print dress. I had an impulse to burst out laughing; it had become utterly ridiculous. Farraday had at least the decency to take Janet's arm and walk with her, and Linda pulled me back and whispered, "What kind of horse's ass are you, Scott!—to bring that kid here? It's your mother. Why are you doing this to her? Do you hate your own mother?"

"I thought—"

"What? Are you going to marry this kid? What could you possibly think?"

I pulled away from her. In the living room, Janet had paused at the grand piano and was staring at the pictures of Martha and me.

"That's Martha with Scott. She was his wife," Mother said.

"I know," Janet agreed. "She was very lovely."

"They were very young," Mother said.

"Yes, I know."

During dinner, Linda prattled on and on about her two daughters, and Farraday complained bitterly about the cost of

147

private school. Then Linda turned the conversation to film. Did Janet ever take a speaking part?

"No, not really. I love to dance—I guess it's my whole life. That happens when you dance. You begin to think and speak with your body, and everything else becomes less important, and when you can't dance, it's a kind of deprivation."

"I look at dance differently now," I said. "Truth is, I never thought of it very much. Now I try to understand it."

"Do you enjoy it, Scott?" Farraday asked.

"I think so." I was breathing a bit more easily now. Janet had not clammed up. She was being as agreeable and charming as ever, and I felt that we might just come out of this without things spoiling. It wasn't until the meal was almost over and the dessert was served that my mother, who had been rather silent, said, apropos of nothing we were talking about, "How did you and Janet come to meet?"

Janet smiled slightly, and before I could reply, she said, "I make my living waiting tables at Jack's. That's a restaurant in the Village, and if I do get a job in a show, he's very good about it. Scott eats there very often, and about two months ago, he picked me up and took me out on a date. I was very grateful, because I had never known anyone like Scott. I mean, being what I am. I am seriously damaged goods, Mrs. Waring. When I was eleven years old, a concentration camp guard raped me. He kept me alive until the concentration camp was liberated, beating me and raping me. I was twelve years old when the camp was liberated. So you can imagine how much it meant to me to have someone like Scott become my friend."

Coffee was being served in the living room. I explained that we were both tired, and since no one had thought of anything much to say after Janet's explanation of how we met, no one objected to our leaving.

The doorman downstairs asked me whether he could get me a cab.

"I'd like to walk for a while," Janet said. "It's a lovely evening, and the air is sweet."

We walked south on Fifth Avenue, and we were almost at 59th Street before either of us spoke; that is, before either of us spoke aloud. I had gone through innumerable silent conversations with myself.

"Did you have to?" I asked her.

"Yes, Scott. I had to."

"Why?"

"Why did you bring me there?"

"I want to marry you."

"Oh, Scott, for heaven's sake, what would that have to do with marrying me?"

"It's a family, and I'm a part of it."

"And you really thought you could make me part of it?"

"Yes," I said strongly. "Yes."

"Scott, I won't marry you."

"Why? Because of tonight? You mean because of what happened tonight? But what has tonight got to do with the fact that I love you?"

"Oh, God, no, not because of tonight! Don't you have any sense of who you are and what you are?"

"I love you."

"God damn you, Scott, you don't love me! You love that wretched damn beautiful blond on the grand piano—a *ménage à trois* with a ghost! No thank you!" She stepped off the sidewalk and hailed a cab, and when I tried to follow her into it, she said, "No thank you. We go home separately tonight."

# IV

*I* went home and sulked. If our relationship meant so little to her, let it be. As I put it down, I find relationship to be a disgusting, misused word, suitable for second cousins and not much more. When I first met Martha Pembroke at the mixer dance between Wellesley and MIT, no one would have described what happened between us as a relationship. We fell in love with each other; but by trying to think about Janet on that night, after the dinner party, I made it a *relationship*. I recall the word because I subsequently spelled it out to Dr. Lieberman, who said, yes, his practice was full of relationships. The next day, sulking no longer filled the void that was beginning to open in my life. I considered going to Jack's for dinner and forcing a meeting, but knowing Janet, I presumed that she had already arranged with Jack to seat me with another waiter, and in my self-pity, I had two frankfurters at a sidewalk pushcart, went home, tried to look at the television I had purchased the week before—Janet and I had curled up on the couch, watching some idiot program, content with being together—found myself irritated, only irritated. I read the newspaper. I opened a copy of the *New Yorker* and studied the cartoons without pleasure or amusement. And I kept looking at my watch, waiting for ten-thirty, when she might be home, and then I contained myself until eleven. I called her at eleven o'clock; no answer. I called at eleven-thirty; no answer.

The next day, having no solution to my condition, I resorted to the practice of numerous red-blooded brainless American males confronted with difficult problems; I got drunk. Finished with my day at the offices of Holben-Chute, where I had spent an endless procession of hours estimating costs on a proposed overpass for a six-lane highway in Michigan, I walked up to Houston Street and Ninth Avenue, where I entered a place called Murphy's Bar. I am not a good drinker. I enjoy wine with dinner, and I'll have a cocktail when I'm with other people having cocktails. I don't drink alone; so this was a contrived decision to get drunk. When I spell out a stupid action in writing, I am always amazed that the stupidity of it did not strike me at the time. I had had nothing to eat since chewing a tasteless ham and cheese sandwich at my desk. I ordered a double martini, drank it and ordered another. I stood at the bar. Two other men stood at the bar, drinking and discussing New York City politics. One of them offered the opinion that the prevailing situation stank.

"It stinks," said his companion, "because we got that brainless wop for a mayor." He was referring to Vincent Impellitteri, then mayor of New York.

"We got the wop because we got the Jews," his friend said.

"That makes no fuckin' sense."

"No? You ask me, that stupid prick is Jewish."

"You're telling me Impellitteri is Jewish?"

"He changed his name. Nobody is mayor unless the fuckin' Jews want him to be."

I had finished my second double martini. "You two," I said, turning to them, "are not only stupid, but you're a pair of brain-damaged, anti-Semitic assholes."

They suspended their political discussion and turned to me. They were large men, probably longshoremen, with heavy shoulders, thick necks and large arms. I had gone through four years of World War Two without ever using my fists, and I couldn't remember the time, even as a kid, when I had punched another human being. My single resort to physical violence occurred when I struck the SS man driving the car in Germany, and that was motivated by desperation; and I might add that I couldn't remember a time when I'd had two double martinis on an empty stomach. One of the men now pointed a finger at me and said, "Asshole, say that again."

Doing my best to stay upright, clenching my fists for the coming battle, I repeated what I had said—that is, more or less. The coming battle was one-sided, and I was too drunk for analysis; but the fact of the matter was that somewhere, in my blurred thinking, I had spent seven weeks being a companion to, and sleeping with, a Jewish girl, and in the course of it I had discovered that my mother did not like Jews. All right, the world is filled with people who do not like Jews. I had found two of them here, and I decided to insult them, and as I was raising my clenched fists to do drunken battle with a moron, the moron hit me. I have no clear memory of what happened after that, but I learned that he hit me several times again, after I had apparently blacked out. I returned to consciousness in the emergency room at St. Vincent's Hospital at Seventh Avenue and 11th Street.

The intern by my bed informed me that I had been beaten severely, that I had a concussion but no fracture of the skull or face, and two broken ribs.

"How do you feel?" he asked me.

I managed to ask him whether he was sure my jaw was not broken.

"Not broken, no. You have all your teeth. That's lucky."

"I'm lucky," I agreed. "Why does it hurt so much?"

"Trauma hurts," he replied, a dumb answer to a dumb question. "You were beaten up in a bar, and they called our ambulance. Who do you want us to notify?"

"No one," I said sourly. "When can I leave?"

"You can't. We have to run some tests. Give it a day or two. Married?"

"No."

A middle-aged woman joined us. "How do you intend to pay for a room?" She had a blue dress and a white apron.

"If I can't pay, you toss me out?"

The woman sighed and shook her head. "She's a sister. She's full of mercy," the intern said. "She won't dump you onto the street. Anyway, you weren't robbed. That's the advantage of being beaten up in a respectable saloon."

They kept me there at St. Vincent's for three days. On the third day, at ten o'clock in the morning, Janet walked into my room. It was a double room, and I was grateful that the other bed was empty. I was out of bed, sitting in a chair, dressed and waiting for a sister to come by with my release papers. Before I could rise, she went to me and kissed me gently, not on my lips but on my forehead.

"How did you know I was here?"

"I decided to be sensible and return all the calls I never answered. I was worried, so I called Holben-Chute. They said you had an accident. An auto accident?" She had brought with her a huge bunch of spring flowers. "Thank God you're all right! What happened to your face?" She put the flowers on the bed, and took off her coat. She was wearing the yellow, long-sleeved top and a grey skirt.

"I was beat up in a bar on Houston Street. They're letting me out today." I was by no means sure of my ground. She was brisk and almost business-like.

"In a fight? You mean you got into a fight?"

"Yes."

"Why, Scott? Why?"

"I was drunk."

She stared at me bewilderedly.

"I'm so glad you came by."

"Why didn't you call me?"

I shrugged. "I tried calling you."

"Can you walk?"

"Of course I can walk. I'm all right. I had a concussion. That's all."

"It's not like you. I can't see you getting drunk and into some stupid barroom squabble."

"It happened."

"And where are you going now?"

"I'll go to the office and lie about it."

"You should," she agreed. "You should certainly lie about it. Does your face hurt?"

"Not much. It just looks awful. Janet," I said, after a moment, "can we have dinner tonight and talk?"

"About what?"

"About you and me and the other night."

"No."

"Then, for Christ's sake, why did you come here?"

"Because I care for you, and because they told me you were hurt."

"I don't understand," I said hopelessly.

She took my hand, holding it in both her hands. "You're a sweet man, Scott, but I don't know who you are. I don't think you know who you are."

# V

So you fucked up again," Dr. Lieberman said to me.

"It's a peculiar kind of medicine you practice, if I may say so."

"I'm not sure it's medicine at all. I don't sell sympathy, but then I'm not sure what I sell. Neurosis is the handiest word the language ever cooked up. The books say that it's something of a functional nervous disease or an emotional disorder, but in this interesting world we inhabit, what isn't? Of course, the two ends of the definition of neurosis are contradictory, but the way we go about dealing with mental problems, that doesn't seem to matter very much. You telephoned me and said you wanted to talk, and we spend an hour together, actually fifty minutes, and I bill you for fifty dollars. If I were a Freudian with a fancy reputation in the business, I'd charge you a hundred or even twice that. I operate under some restraints and some guilts."

"Can you help me?"

"I'll try. I like you."

"I've never seen much evidence of it," I said.

"I do my best. Tell me, why don't you marry her?"

"She wouldn't have me."

"Come on, Scott, this is the moment of truth. Did you ask her? Did you say, Look here, Janet, let's go down to City Hall and get ourselves married?"

I considered that before I answered. "No."

"And when you brought her to your mother's house, did you anticipate what would happen?"

I struggled with that one, and Dr. Lieberman said, after a minute or two, "Why don't you lie down? It's easier to work out that kind of thing if you're not looking at me."

"OK, sure." I stretched out on the couch.

"That's the hardest question in the world," he said, "why was it done? A man murders someone. He's asked why. His whole life hangs in the balance, but he can't say why. You read it in the papers every day."

"You want me to say—"

"I don't want you to say anything. I get paid the same whether you lie there in silence or whether you talk."

"You're being real pleasant today." No response to that. "You want me to say that I took her to my mother's house because I knew that it would put an end to any possibility of my marrying her."

"God be praised, I don't want you to say anything. Can't you understand that?"

"Yes, damn you!" I shouted. "I can understand it. I took her there because I couldn't face marrying a woman who had been raped at age eleven by some filthy SS bastard and for a whole year was his toy in that stinking Dachau!"

When another long minute or two went by without any comment from Lieberman, I said, my voice breaking and close to tears, "Pin a fucking medal on yourself, doctor."

"Do you want some water?"

"No!"

"Shall we continue? And let me say that before you went into the army, you never would have dared to adopt fuckin' as your favorite adjective. It's worth thinking about."

"Jesus God, didn't you just tell me that I fucked up again?"

"That's different. I select my speech according to my patient. I wasn't being critical. Fuck is a fine old Anglo-Saxon word, which once was a homely expression for the most delightful thing men and women can do. Now it's taboo among the kind of people you come from. And since you've become some kind of ersatz Jew, I might mention that there's no equivalent for it in Yiddish."

"Don't give me that. I'm no kind of a Jew, ersatz or otherwise, and if you weren't being critical, what in hell were you being?"

"Complimentary. I regard it as a breakthrough. And if I were taping this and ran the tape for some of my colleagues in this witchcraft I practice, they'd have me thrown out and force me to be an honest physician again. That might be a good thing. Do you want to continue?"

I thought about it. I'd had enough of him, and my every instinct told me to get up and walk out and once and for all see the end of this sardonic, superior Jew—and then, in a way that had never happened before, I was sick with myself, because in my mind, mixed in all the garbage of a lifetime, he was not Lieberman the psychiatrist, but Lieberman the Jew.

"Yes," I said.

"Good. I want you to talk about Martha."

"Why? Martha's dead. Martha's gone."

"Is she?"

"I know what that means. Janet put it to me flatly. She told me she had no intentions of being part of a *ménage à trois* with a ghost. And I am sick and tired of everyone telling me what's in my head."

"This is a difficult moment for you, Scott," Dr. Lieberman said, a note of kindness in his voice. "Let's try to work with it. If Martha had not died—what were your plans?"

"That's hard to say."

"No. You had plans. You talked about them."

"I guess they were just ordinary plans, we wanted to have three children. I had talked about an apartment in New York, but Martha liked the thought of a house in the country, Westchester or Connecticut. She loved dogs. We were going to have two Irish Setters."

"You were both still in college. How do you go about buying a house in the country? When I went into the service, I had the clothes on my back and a wristwatch."

"Where are we going, doctor?"

"You know where we're going, Scott. Tell me about the house in the country."

"There was no house in the country. Martha died." I paused and said, "I resent this."

"Oh, Lord, may the spirit of Ziggie save us! I had a Catholic patient—they're the toughest—and he was in sin every time he came here, and I used to say Jesus Christ every time I got annoyed, and he would take umbrage. So I tried to break the habit and invoke the spirit of our beloved Sigmund. Scott, you're too damned proud to take any money from your rich mother, and you can't afford to spend a year on my couch. So let's stop the bullshit."

I got off the couch.

"Leaving?"

"No, I'm not leaving." I dropped into a chair. "It's not that I don't know where you're going. I am not totally an idiot. It's just that I exist in a lasting fog of confusion."

"It's not uncommon."

"Why in God's name did I have myself circumcised? Can you tell me that? Can you tell me why I'd do an insane thing like that?"

"I could make a good guess, but I'm not going to." He nodded, which on his part was a gesture of sympathy. "I know I don't work like other shrinks. Maybe it's all the years I spent as a surgeon. We've been at this for the given fifty minutes, but I'm ready to sacrifice my lunch hour."

161

"That's noble of you."

"Let's go back to the house in the country."

"OK. The house in the country was to be the gift of Martha's mother." I took a deep breath.

"That's quite a gift, considering that it was nineteen thirty-nine. The depression was still with us."

"The Pembrokes are rich. They could afford it."

"I gathered as much. A house in Connecticut, two Irish Setters, three bright, beautiful blond children—"

"For Christ's sake!"

He stared at me thoughtfully. "Scott," he said, "we pretend, here in America, that there's no class structure. You're smart enough to know that's a carefully fostered illusion. You and Martha were the golden children of two well-educated white Protestant families. The whole world was yours, and you were raised and trained to politely accept that fact. Then something happened to you. Your beautiful young wife who, like you, had been protected and nurtured to whatever degree our civilization could provide, was brutally murdered by a gang of thugs. You had coddled yourself with your pacifist beliefs, and you found yourself in a war, a monstrous, terrible war. Hans Bauman told me something about your time in the war. You took a demolition crew into a river to blow up a bridge, and under enemy fire. Three men working alongside of you were killed. Then you saw Buchenwald." He paused and waited.

"Your life was saved by a Jewish brothel-keeper," he said, after a long moment.

"Yes—"

"And then you came home. Tell me about that."

"I came home."

"How? How did you come home? What happened?"

"You mean how, physically? How I traveled?"

"Exactly."

"I told you once."

"Tell me again," Lieberman said. "Lie down, please. I want you to recreate it for me. Close your eyes. Live through it again."

I did as he suggested. I lay down on the couch and closed my eyes: "It was a Victory ship, an armed freighter converted into a troop carrier. We packed the rails as the ship came into the harbor. There was the Statue of Liberty. It was very moving. Some of the kids began to cry. Then, as I learned, we got radio orders to drop anchor in the harbor and wait for Immigration to come on board. But the winches weren't working properly, and the harbor master ordered us to continue on and dock at one of the big piers, I think it was in the Forties. We were all packed and waiting with our duffles and valpacks. I had been commissioned major by then—"

"A field commission, wasn't it?"

"Yes, sir." It's amazing how one falls back, yes, sir, no, sir, simply talking about the army.

"A field commission is a great honor, Scott."

"That's bullshit and you know it. Anyway, Immigration came on board, and there I was with my gold cluster, and I

slipped twenty dollars into the Immigration man's hand—
the going price for a quick getaway—and he hardly looked at
my papers, only said, Yes, major, right down the gangway
there, and it was a beautiful, warm sunny October day, about
two o'clock in the afternoon, and I walked the length of the
pier, and there were the cabs lined up on the street. They
were big, beautiful cabs in those days—remember the Waters
cabs?—and I got into the cab, tossed in my valpack, and told
him to take me to my mother's apartment on East Seventy-
second Street. I took a cigar out of my blouse pocket—believe
it or not, the army provided expensive Cuban cigars for the
VIP counters, put up my feet on one of the folding chairs,
and told the driver to cut into the park at Fifty-ninth and
Sixth. I clipped the end, lit the cigar and prepared to be
one of the most fortunate men of the moment—" My voice
died away. I wanted to leave it there. The thought crossed
my mind that it would be something indeed to have a long
delicious dinner with Janet, and then to light a cigar.
People have different and often odd reactions to cigars.
Some hate them, the taste and smell of them. Others like
them. Janet's father had smoked cigars, and when I smoked a
cigar in her presence, it produced sad but warm memories.

"Go on," Lieberman said.

"It was the women—it was a warm day, too warm for coats,
and the women were still in their summer dresses, and there
were kids in the playgrounds, and women pushing baby carriages—oh, Jesus God, I just went to pieces. I threw the cigar

out of the open window and I began to cry. The cabbie pulled over and asked me whether I was in trouble. I was in trouble."

Lieberman was silent, and I left the couch for the chair. Lieberman pushed the box of tissues over to me, and I dried my eyes. "Do you want a drink?" he asked.

"Yes."

He took a bottle of brandy out of his desk and poured a shot glass. The brandy went down like hot fire, and I doubled over, coughing.

"Water?" Lieberman asked.

"No, I'm all right."

"Good. You know, Scott, when I was operating in North Africa, I took some shrapnel out of a lieutenant in the Rangers. You remember the Rangers?"

"Yes, I do."

"They were the one crack unit we had when we went into North Africa, maybe the only real A-one outfit in the army at the time. They were thrown away like waste paper, and they took awful casualties, but they were good. This lieutenant told me about the replacements. They always needed replacements, and he said that a dozen replacements would come in, and he could look at them, and he could pretty well guess who would live and who would die in the next encounter."

"I don't know where this goes," I complained. "I think I don't know what in hell I'm doing here."

"Who would live and who would die. Think about it."

My mind had been off in another direction; I was still with the cab in Central Park. But perhaps that was not another direction at all. I wondered what his little tale of the Rangers had to do with me, and why had I come crawling back to Lieberman? Certainly, no one could equal him in creating in my mind a feeling of total self-disgust. I could not shake loose from the belief that tears in a grown man were a measure of weakness. I was weak enough and confused enough; I didn't need additional proof.

"Go back to Martha," he said. "Talk about her."

"Why?"

"Because your Janet was right. You can't have both."

"How did your man in the Rangers know who would live and who would die?"

"Ask Janet."

"Oh, the hell with it!" I got up and started to go. He made no move to stop me. At the door I paused and said, "I'm sorry."

"For what?"

"You tried to help me."

He shrugged. "I gave you a sort of diploma. You didn't have to come back here, and I guess I shouldn't have let you come back. I think we're friends in some kind of cockeyed way. So just as a friend and not as your witch-doctor, let me leave this with you. If I had a woman like your Janet, I'd break my ass to be with her. She was right. You don't have one damn notion of who you are, but maybe the money spent here opened some doors. I think so."

166

# Part Three

# *Munich*

# I

Whatever else my mother was, to me she was my mother, and for the thirty-five years I had lived, she had been a caring mother, as she saw it. She knew little of what had happened to me during the years away from her; like so many sons—and daughters, I suppose—I sheltered her, as I saw it, from my innermost dreams and agonies; and I carefully sorted out what experiences I would share with her.

There is nothing remarkable about this, and I would suppose she drew the same veil of silence over her experience. Has she been in love with other men than my father? Had she slept with other men before or since his death? Had she deeply loved him? She was a tall, full-bodied and handsome woman. How many men had come on to her? How had she reacted? I knew none of this, nor did I particularly care. Thus it came as no surprise to me that she was totally unaware of what had happened that Sunday night at her home, and in all fairness I must say that possibly I would have been equally insensitive if the situation had been reversed.

She telephoned me a week later to inform me that Alicia Pembroke, Martha's younger sister, was to be married. As my mother put it, "Thank God. The child's twenty-six years old, come this summer, and poor Sally was at her wit's end." Sally was Martha's mother. "And it's a fine boy, same age as Alicia, Harvard Law School and he's with Sam Pembroke's firm in the city. He's from Hartford, Jefferson Benton, and all in all, Sally Pembroke's happy as a summer lark."

"Yes, Mother."

"June twelfth, at the Congregational Church in Southport. It's sudden, so the invitations are late. The wedding's at four, and then cocktails and dinner at their club. I'll expect you to be my escort—and a very handsome one."

"Mother—"

"Scott, you're not going to decline this."

"Actually, Mother, I'd like to plead out of this."

"Scott, how could you!"

That was reasonable enough. How could I? Almost as an afterthought, she said, "Are you still seeing that little dark girl, the one from the concentration camp?"

Linda called the same day and asked me to lunch with her. I repeated what my mother had said. "Scott, Scott," Linda replied, "what else could you have expected? Mother is Mother." Linda, tall, beautiful, her hair carefully restored to the color it was when she was sixteen, wearing a suit that had cost at least a thousand dollars, was just enough removed from my mother to be her and yet not be her.

"You must go," she instructed me. "There is no way you can not go. The Pembrokes look upon you as a son. I know you've neglected them, but you're their compensation for the loss of Martha. I can't imagine why it should be so painful for you. Surely, you still think of Martha."

"Yes, I still think of Martha."

"I can't imagine," Linda said, "why you decided to bring—what's her name?—why you decided to introduce her to Mother."

"Janet is her name. It was only last week, Linda."

"Yes, I'm bad with names. I'm sure she's a lovely person. She's bright enough. Were you thinking of marrying her?"

"The truth is that I'm leaving for Germany the following day, and that makes it a very tight thing."

"Germany? For heaven's sake, why would you go to Germany?"

"I need a vacation. The auto accident shook me up, and I have a few weeks of vacation time coming to me."

"Poor dear!" Linda was all sympathy. The truth is that we were close as kids growing up, and Linda reached over to touch my face very gently. "Thank God it was only a concussion, and a little pancake would cover the bruises. Men never think of such things. But Germany? That's a hateful place, and after what happened to Martha and your time there during the war—well, I just can't imagine why you should want to go back there?"

"Curiosity."

"Oh, come on, Scott! That poor child last week—well, after hearing her story—"

"Bad things happen. They happen here too."

"Still, you say it's the day after the wedding, and that doesn't prevent you from coming." She leaned across the table and took my hand. "Scott, if you're not there, well, Mother and I won't be able to explain—please."

I sighed and nodded. "OK, I'll bring Mother."

"And please, please don't talk about going to Germany. I know you are fluent in the language, and I suppose it's an ego thing to go into another country and speak their language. I love Paris partly because I love the language, but France isn't Germany, is it? Sally Pembroke just wouldn't know what to make of it."

I saw Dr. Lieberman the following day. I had done a lot of thinking after seeing him, and I reflected on my behavior and decided that it was abominable. That night, I sat alone in my apartment, chewing on a sandwich and sipping at a bottle of beer and staring at the photograph of Martha that had taken Janet's attention. Almost fifteen years had gone by, and staring at the photograph now I felt an uneasy sense of strangeness, of disassociation. I opened a drawer where I kept the snapshots of Martha and myself, pictures taken by her father and mother, by my sister and by others whose name and presence I had forgotten, Martha and I on a sailing skiff, sitting beside a lake, at a tennis court, holding hands and mugging at the camera, in a canoe, sprawled out on a deck in our bathing suits; and there were the pictures I had taken of Martha alone, dozens of them, Martha in every pose, in the bright yellow dress that was my summer favorite, in shorts, in a bathing suit; and there were the wedding pictures. Some I looked at for long moments; others I tossed aside with hardly a glance; and finally, I put all of them together in a pile on the coffee table. I took the large portrait out of its frame and added it to the pile, and then I sat and studied the pile of photographs and tried to evoke the feeling I had when she was alive and we were together.

I couldn't. There was a pile of photographs of a stranger, and the very presence of such a thought chilled my blood. I tried to reclaim her, this sweet and lovely woman whom I had adored, but I groped through memories as devoid of reality as dead leaves. Closing my eyes, I tried to visualize her, but the only memory I could evoke was of the room in the Gestapo house and the one-way mirror through which I watched her being beaten.

Out of a sudden impulse, I called Dr. Lieberman at his home and asked him whether I could take him to dinner.

"A sort of farewell dinner? You don't have to coddle your guilts, Scott."

"I'd just like to talk to you outside of that wretched office of yours."

"Why not? Shall I bring my wife?"

"I'd love to meet her, but not this time. Just the two of us."

"Fine."

I told him the place, and he agreed to meet me there the following evening. Then I returned to contemplation of the pile of photographs.

"Suppose I burn them?"

I could do Lieberman almost as well as Lieberman. "Do they threaten you?"

"No, they remind me."

"She died once, long ago. She doesn't have to die again." No, that was not vintage Lieberman, he was never that specific. "You can love her and you can love another." Just too damn silly to be Lieberman. I put the pictures away in the drawer, and for the first time I said to myself, words to this effect, It's good to think about her. She was young and beautiful and filled with sunlight, and she'll always be that way. Good-bye, my darling.

It was an interesting change to face Dr. Lieberman across the table in a brightly lit restaurant, apart from his natural habitat and his black leather couch. He actually wore a white shirt, a red tie and a gray flannel suit, and for the first time I thought of him as a rather good-looking man—or perhaps simply as another man. "Tonight," I said, "I have decided to call you Max. I've been very respectful, but tonight—do you mind?"

"Not at all."

We ordered our dinner, and when I added a thirty-dollar bottle of wine, he asked whether this was a celebratory occasion. "If it is, what are we celebrating?"

"A gift, and gratitude. I intend not to see you again, unless you invite former patients to dinner at your home or some such social thing."

"I usually don't. I might make an exception."

"I stormed out of your office yesterday in a fine fury. I spent part of the evening with photos of Martha. I remembered some good things and some bad things. I love her very much. I will always love her. That was new. Do I make any sense?"

"Enlighten me more."

"I think I love Janet. I was able to remember Martha. I don't love her any less."

The waiter had opened the bottle of wine, and now he poured it.

"Do I make any sense?" I asked him again.

He nodded. "We can drink to that. Maybe there's something in this witch-doctor racket of mine."

"The gratitude is to you. I've been a lousy patient."

"All my patients are lousy patients," Lieberman said, raising his glass. "It goes with the trade. You make me feel good, Scott. We'll drink to both of us. What about Janet? Have you seen her?"

"Not today."

"Are you going to marry her?"

"If she'll have me. There are still one or two things I have to work out. I'm going back to Germany."

His reaction was unexpected. He smiled at me. Evidently,

where his patients were concerned, Lieberman treasured his smiles and used them rarely.

"You're not surprised?"

"There's a tired story every shrink uses. A man on the street crawls around under a lamppost. A passerby asks him what he's looking for. The key for my car, he says. Did you drop it here? No, the crawler replies. I dropped it up the street. But it's dark up there and it's light here."

"You told me that one months ago."

Lieberman shrugged. "A good story bears repeating."

"I suppose so. Martha's young sister is being married. They want me at the wedding."

"Are you going?"

"I think so—yes."

"That's good. A month ago—"

"I wouldn't have gone. You're right."

"It's a breakthrough. I'm glad. And your face looks better."

"Courtesy of my sister, Linda. She suggested pancake makeup."

"Did you tell her that you were beat up in a bar for being more stupid than anyone has a right to be?"

"No, I told her I was in an auto accident. Furthermore, I admit to being drunk. But do you regard it as stupid to take exception to anti-Semitism?"

"Yes. I'm Jewish. If I started a fight every time I heard a piece of anti-Semitism, I'd be a basket case by now. And just in terms of your general education, two heavyweight boxers and two Olympic wrestlers were once asked what they would do if they were insulted in a bar, and all four of them said they'd turn around and walk out. You went through a long, terrible war, and you saw men killed, but believe me, nothing that happened to you was as dangerous as what you did the other night. Let me tell you something about Jews. There is one thing that most Jews learn, and if they don't learn it, they pay a large price. That's survival."

"Yes, and six million of you died in the Holocaust."

"That's the large price. And when you get to Germany, don't start any new wars. Just use your head."

All in all, it was a decently pleasant dinner. I felt I owed it to him.

John Farraday's chauffeur picked up my mother and me at the apartment on 72nd Street. Linda wore a long, black satin coat over a gray silk dress. My mother wore pink. Farraday and I were in white dinner jackets. The Congregational Church in Southport was filled with people properly dressed and restrainedly enthusiastic. Alicia was beautiful, so like Martha in figure and coloring that my heart skipped a beat. Sally Pembroke embraced me and wept. Sam Pembroke shook my hand warmly. Mother embraced Alicia and wept and ruined her eye makeup and had to dash to shelter to repair it. The dinner at the Pembroke's club was modest and restrained, and the bridegroom was tall and handsome. I was introduced to a very good-looking young woman who informed me that she had been at school with Martha, married and divorced since then, and lived in New York on East 63rd Street. Sally Pembroke said to me, "Scott, I feel that Martha is here with us. Don't you?" I said that I did. The lady from East 63rd Street asked me to dance with her, and I begged off, pleading that I was a rotten dancer. Linda was furious with me, because after that, I couldn't dance with my mother. Sam Pembroke said to me, "You win some, you lose some, Scott. When you do marry, bring your bride to us. Do you understand?" I said that I understood. They were nice, sympathetic, decent people, and Sam Pembroke was a little drunk. Only to be expected. I was a little drunk myself.

We dropped my mother off at her apartment. Linda offered her chauffeur to drive me home, but I preferred to walk. It was a cool, pleasant June evening, and the East Side streets were almost empty. As I walked, the effects of the liquor wore off and I was filled with an overwhelming desire to stop at one of the public telephones and call Janet. I was able to resist. My plane was taking off at ten o'clock the following morning, and I felt to call her now would be utterly senseless. She would ask me, providing she spoke to me, why I was going to Germany. That was not anything I cared to explain to anyone.

# II

The guidebooks tend to wax ecstatic over Munich —"Where the light and rosy joy of Bavaria replaces the seriousness of Northern Germany." "Where music and joy give a city its character." "Where beer flows like a golden river." "Where civilization's noblest achievements, such as the Alte Pinakothek, thrive and flourish."

Few guidebooks are literary gems, and none of them mention Adolf Hitler, who also did business in Munich. My first intimation of Munich came on the plane from London, where I stopped briefly to do a most unusual thing: that is, the plane I took had a scheduled four-hour stop there, and I used some of the time to purchase and mail a box of excellent cigars to Dr. Max Lieberman. I mention this because all across the Atlantic—the first time I had ever made a transoceanic trip by air—I was trying to work out whether I simply hated the man or might just be everlastingly grateful to him. The cigars were the result, not of decision, but of indecision.

When the plane took off for Munich, the empty seat next

to me had been filled by a young man in his late twenties or so, well-dressed, indeed rather elegantly. "My name is Kurt Vonelde," he said in excellent English. "I hope you don't mind my taking this seat?"

"Not at all."

"They seated me next to a fat, Bavarian pig. It was impossible, if you will forgive me?"

"There is nothing to forgive. The seat was empty," I replied, speaking German in response to his accent.

"Oh, my God," he said. "Allow me to apologize. I thought you were an American, and here I've been a perfect ass, and I pray you're not Bavarian."

"I'm an American."

"Thank goodness. I don't know what to say or how to explain. I'm Prussian, so we have an attitude about Bavarians." He was speaking German now, the hard, precise German of the North. "But your German? You hardly have an accent."

"I had it in school. I'm an engineer. In my country, when you're in the humanities, you study French. When you're in engineering, you study German. And then I was in the army."

"As I was."

"My name is Scott Waring." He offered his hand, and I took it. He was pleasant, elegant, with the attitude of a well-brought-up Englishman, the attitude that says, I can see that you too are a gentleman, so we can talk.

"Delighted, Herr Waring. Are you here on business?"

"In a manner of speaking."

"Of course, it's none of my affair. I am back and forth between London and Munich. I sell beer. You see, my family lived in Prussia, where we grew apples and had tenant farmers and all the other nonsense that goes with being Prussian gentry. But now Prussia is Poland, and I make a decent living selling Bavarian beer to the British. The fortunes of war, as they say."

"Yes, but you don't care for Bavarians?"

"I'm afraid not." He thought about it for a moment, and then added, "Of course, there are decent and pleasant Bavarians, and Munich can be a charming city—not Berlin or Paris, but quite charming for being stuck away in the middle of the mountains. Have you been there before?"

"Just for a day, and it was battered at the time. A lot of smashed buildings. You know, it was quite extraordinary how few competent German speakers we had. I was with an engineering unit, but I was pulled out again and again as an interpreter." Quite deliberately, I continued, "The need was greatest when we liberated the camps. There were all these poor devils, the few thousand who were survivors, desperate to talk, to exchange a word. I went into Buchenwald when it was first liberated. That was enough. Then I was ordered to Munich after Dachau was liberated. They had quartered a few hundred of the survivors in Munich, in what they called the Residenz—"

I was interrupted by the arrival of tea and tiny British tea sandwiches. My seat companion had listened thoughtfully.

*

Now he said, "Yes, Herr Waring, the old palace of the Duke of Wittelsbach, I know the place."

I chewed a sandwich of butter and watercress, and closed my eyes for a moment, and recalled a thin, withered old Jewish man in his striped concentration camp clothes. I say old, but possibly he was in his forties or fifties. When your teeth fall out and your flesh hangs on your bones, age exists without time. I was making notes for destination, and I asked him where he wished to be sent. "New Zealand," he answered sadly. "But it's so far," I said, and he said to me, "From where, Herr American?"

We sat in silence for a while, busy with our tea and sandwiches, Vonelde either lost in his own thoughts or silenced by my reference to the concentration camps. When the tea things were taken away, Vonelde said, "I spend a good deal of time in Great Britain," speaking English now, "and I work on my German accent all the time. That's a sort of curious guilt. I suppose I would rather not be taken for German, and I buy my clothes on Bond Street and have them measured and made to order. That's a silly business. I could buy them for half the price here in Germany. I don't know why I'm talking about this at all. We make almost a religion about never mentioning the war or the Nazis, because as demented as it sounds, we're very civilized people."

"I think I understand that," I said.

"It's the camps, Waring. I meet someone like you, and I really don't give a bloody damn whether you think we're a bloody lot of barbarians or not, and then the thing about the camps comes up. I don't know you from Adam, sir."

"No, you don't."

He lapsed into silence after that, and I picked up my newspaper and made a try at reading it. About fifteen minutes went by, and then Vonelde said, "I had no business being rude."

"I didn't feel you were rude."

"You see, Waring, I commanded a machine gun unit in Russia. Eighteen men. I survived. The other seventeen are buried somewhere in Russia. My father was General Gert Vonelde. He was a member of the General Staff. He was convicted in the plot against Hitler, and he was shot by firing squad."

We were silent for the rest of the trip, and when we landed in the Munich-Riem Airport, we shook hands. I never saw Vonelde again. I liked him, but on the other hand, I felt no sympathy for him or his father. His father had a quick, easy death, which is more or less what one expects in that profession, and while "Bavarian pigs" made him uncomfortable, he seemed to be making a perfectly good living selling their beer.

The fact of the matter is that Munich surprised me. Only eight years had gone by, yet most of the ruins were gone, rebuilt, replaced. The city was clean and bright and alive— and, amazingly, had become a sort of center for teen-age kids, handsome, well-fed blond youngsters who were everywhere, on vacation, hiking in their short leather pants, filling the beer halls.

I spent three days in Munich. I put up at the Grand Hotel, where the help reached new levels of obsequious service. When my excellent German was praised, I explained that I was Jewish and that German was close enough to Yiddish, and I found myself taking a malevolent satisfaction in the silly deception. I actually did not know two words of Yiddish. Dr. Lieberman, in his own inimitable manner, had advised me to stop being a horse's ass and trying to turn myself into a Jew out of some idiot goyish desire for absolution, and to concentrate on finding out who Scott Waring actually was; yet I had a feeling that this charade would not irritate him. Curiously enough, this business of pretending to be Jewish only made the people I encountered more obsequious and over-polite. Nothing in my life has ever confused me and bewildered me as much as the inner life of Germans, their cloying politeness, their incredible energy in rebuilding and transforming this ruined city, and their insistence, shared by everyone I spoke to, that not only were they never Nazis, but that they had hated the Nazis from start to finish. Yet I could not share Vonelde's belittling opinion of the Bavarians. Munich throbbed with energy, and if I could have looked at it objectively, I would have seen it as an amazing city, so much more amazing than Berlin.

I had come to Munich with only one purpose in mind, to try to enter the soul of a little girl who had been put into Dachau at age eleven, and if that sounds vague and even somewhat preposterous, it is because my motivations were equally vague. I had my own battleground, and an effort to spell it out properly defeats me; except that somehow I had come to understand that I was fighting for my own immortal soul—whether or not there was such a thing—and either I would find my own peculiar salvation or live the rest of my life "entirely fucked up" as Lieberman phrased it in his interesting brand of psychological terminology.

I cursed myself for not having asked Janet Goldman what street she had lived on. I had thought it might be Bayerstrasse because she spoke of a park nearby, but going there, I decided it could not have been; and then I tried Brienner Strasse but could find nothing resembling the house she had described. She had mentioned sitting with her father in a cafe in Schwabing. I found a sidewalk cafe there in the old art center, which was their poor attempt to imitate Paris, and I sat with a glass of wine, sipping it in the delightful June sunshine and making a fantasy of her being here with me. A large, buxom blond woman replaced my fantasy and told me in broken English that she could give me a lovely time for five dollars American. In German, I told her that she could have the rest of my bottle of wine, already paid for, and we parted amicably.

I spent most of the day at the Alte Pinakothek, which means Old Picture Place. From the time Janet was seven or eight years old, her father had taken her to the Alte Pinakothek, telling her how lucky they were to live here in Munich, where any time they desired, they could go and look at the pictures. Many of the old Dutch and Flemish paintings are of a pre-Renaissance era, and they appear to float in a mysterious world beyond reality; and it's one of the many incomprehensible contradictions of Germany that this collection of delicate, sensitive paintings—a collection matched nowhere else on earth—should exist in the city that gave rise to the Nazi movement.

Janet had told me the story of her father pointing out to her a portrait of the Christ. "Look at it," he had said to her. It was a portrait of a Jew in agony, a face unmistakably Jewish—if there is such a thing. She had mentioned the painting several times, and I moved through the museum, searching every painting, until I found it. It was unmistakable—and indeed among all the portraits of Jesus I have ever seen, only this one made me feel that I was looking at the face of the man on the cross—yet the portrait was not of a man on a cross, but only the head and shoulders of a man with a crown of thorns.

I know that many men and women have gone through a set of experiences not dissimilar to mine over the past decade, indeed a whole generation have lived through it; but each sees it and lives it in his own way; and here now, I had the feeling of a little child's hand in mine.

A voice asked, "Are you all right, sir?"

I realized that my cheeks were covered with tears. A small, white-haired lady stood beside me, and as I wiped my eyes, she said in German, "It's all right. Very often, when I come here and look at that painting, I cry. I look at it and I feel that the whole world is crying." She paused and touched the sleeve of my jacket, and said in broken English, "You are not German?"

"I speak German," I said. "I'm an American."

"Ah, so. I live here in Munich."

"Yes?"

"I am Jewish," she said. "You are not Jewish?"

"No."

"Where do you come from?"

"New York."

She was a very gentle person, not aggressive, almost apologetic with her soft voice.

"There are so many Jews in New York, it seems impossible. There are very few Jews here in Munich, almost none."

"Have you always lived in Munich?" I asked her.

"I was born here. My husband was a doctor. I had two sons and a daughter. My husband sent her to Switzerland, and now she lives in Italy. They took my husband and my two sons. A Christian family sheltered me."

"Perhaps you knew a family called Goldman?"

She shook her head. "I don't think so."

She wandered off then. I had thought of asking her why she remained here in Munich. I can guess what she might have said—"Where should I go? Here I have the language."

Would my own life have been better, worse, different, if I had not had the German language? Different, certainly.

I had an impulse to go after her and say to her, "Tell me

about the Christian family that sheltered you." You think of a
thing like that when the moment has passed, and instead I
remained staring at the painting of the tortured Jewish Christ.

I love good beer. That evening, I went to a beer hall, and
ate veal sausage and liver sausage and drank beer and smoked
a cigar, while the handsome youngsters around me toasted
each other and sang songs and fondled each other—the children
of fathers who had murdered in their camps six million Jews and
two million Russians and Poles and a million Gypsies and almost a million of their own people, good Christians who had
made the mistake of being communists, socialists, or simply
anti-Nazi. It was an interesting city in an interesting country.

The next day, I checked out of the hotel, rented a Ford, and
drove to Dachau. You would think of it in some wretched
morass, or on a piece of dirty mud or in some burned
meadow, but it isn't. It's lovely countryside, sweet and green.
The town nearby is terraced and quaint, but there's nothing
quaint about the camp. It consists of 32 white, black-roofed
barracks, laid out neatly in two rows, the whole of it surrounded by a wire fence, electrified when it was in use as a
concentration camp. Over the gate, painted neatly: *Arbeit
Macht Frei,* work will make you free. The guards were given
the right to shoot anyone who stepped closer than three feet
to the wire fence, and this was fine sport for the sporting SS
men. Dachau was, indeed, a training school for SS guards,
and before the war ended 150 smaller imitations of Dachau
were established all over Germany. Dachau was famous for its

scientific studies, and there were two smaller white buildings where the doctors carried on their dissection of living people, where they transplanted organs and where they investigated how long a Jew or a Pole could live as piece by piece his brain was removed. Dachau could not match the great murder camps, like Auschwitz, where a million and a half Jews were put to death, or Treblinka, where seven hundred and fifty thousand Jews were murdered; less than a hundred thousand died at Dachau.

I parked my car outside the main gate. Dachau is about eighteen miles from Munich, and it was still rather early in the morning. Only a dozen or so cars were parked in the field outside the main gate, and there was a cluster of middle-aged men waiting, wearing armbands which identified them as guides. Their rejection of Nazism in broken English was a common chorus. I handed one of them an American dollar and he almost groveled with gratitude. I told him to use German.

"Ah, then you are German? A Prussian?"

"American."

"Ah, so—yes, of course. We go through the gate. Above the gate—work will make you free. A cruel deception. The poor souls here were worked to death. Only death made them free. What a scar on our national honor! But we must look at the past and remember. Thank God I was a soldier, drafted into the army. Not a Nazi, never. The Americans who come here think we were all Nazis. But what is a man to do? You follow orders, otherwise the firing squad. You were in the army yourself, perhaps?"

"Where were the SS men quartered?"

"Your German is excellent, excellent. In that house, over there. And that small house—that is where the doctors did their devilish work. It was a thing of horror. We go into the barracks. I see you don't have a camera. I have a camera." He took it out of his jacket pocket. "I can take a roll of film for you. Then I give you the roll and you can have it developed— only five dollars American. Yes, Herr American?"

"No. No pictures."

"Yes. Yes, of course. As you wish. We go into the barracks. It is a pleasure to talk to a tourist in German. English is a very hard language."

We went into a long building, and as we entered, the guide flicked a switch to light up the dismal place, a testament to German efficiency. As in Buchenwald, the room was lined with wooden bunks, floor to ceiling. The place smelled of astringent cleaning fluid, as if the scent of death was impossible to exclude.

In my mind's eye, I see her, a little child of eleven years. An SS guard takes her by the hand and leads this skinny, shivering child to his quarters. He orders her to take off her ragged dress. She stands mute, the tears running down her cheeks, then he tears off the dress, and the small body is revealed naked. He orders her to lie down on the bed. Then he undresses, boastfully exhibiting his proud penis to the terrified child, and then he rapes her, tearing her hymen, injecting her with the sperm of the master race, waving his bloody prick in supreme Aryan pride, while she lies broken and bleeding. And he keeps her. He is filled with human generosity and compassion, so he does not send this child along with her mother and father and sisters and brother in transport to Auschwitz to the gas extinction chamber. He keeps her, so that he can rape her again and again, as the mood takes him. He is a tall, handsome man, with a head of fine blond hair and bright blue eyes, and when he visits the local brothel in the pretty picture-postcard town of Dachau, the whores scramble for his attention. That is very pleasant, but the little Jewish girl he keeps in his quarters is something special, his very own virgin whom he deflowered and whom no other man ever touched. He has let it be known among his comrades that if anyone so much as lays a finger on his little Jew, he will pay the price. When he visits the brothel in Dachau, and leaves his whore with his immediate lust gratified, feeling all relaxed and easy, he will buy a box of chocolates or a pastry for his little Jew. He teaches her to polish his boots, to shine the brass buttons on his black uniform coat, to wash his shirts and socks. If she weeps too much, a single blow with the back of his hand quiets her. She knows that he does not enjoy the sight of her tears or the sound of her whimpers, so gradually she learns to control her horror and terror. Not that it ever becomes less, but she learns to control it. The SS man becomes used to her presence. He will fall asleep, leaving his Luger pistol in the holster in plain view of the child. But she cannot kill him, not a man, not even a mouse, and the life force in her is too strong for her to kill herself. As all things come to an end, so does this come to an end, and one day, through the window of her room, she sees the American troops pour into the camp. Her captor has disappeared. It is over.

"This," my guide informed me, "was the women's barracks. You see, they had real toilets, not the slop pails that were provided for the men's barracks. You can relieve yourself here, if you wish. The toilets are clean." He could not keep a note of pride out of his voice. The toilets were clean.

Outside, in the sweet summer sunshine that God grants us, so that His children may grow and flourish, the guard said to me, "I trust you have enjoyed your visit, Herr American. I try to be informative. I think that is the purpose of a good guide, is that not so?"

I walked to my rented car and sat down behind the wheel. The Ford was a European model, and I tried to recall whether Ford had opened a factory in the New Germany. After all, the world was a small place, and no country had ever recovered from a war fought on its own territory as quickly as Germany. In fact, you could drive through Germany on the great *Autobahns* and never see any sign of the war.

# III

In Dachau, I loaded my car with food. I had decided to drive to Coburg, and from there to Frankfurt, where I would board a plane for home. I didn't know what the food situation might be in Coburg, but Dachau was a tourist town and well-stocked. I bought two smoked hams, yards of sausage, an assortment of canned goods, oranges, potatoes, five pounds of butter, several cabbages and a case of beer. Dachau to Coburg was about 180 miles, an easy drive through rolling hills and prosperous farm country. It was early evening when I pulled off the road alongside Berthe Baum's house.

I had given her no warning that I was coming. I didn't know, in all truth, whether she was alive or dead, living in the same house or elsewhere; but I felt that even if she had gone, it was a small effort to make this trip. In eight years, much can happen, but the house was in good shape, the shell damage repaired. She must have heard the car, because she had opened the front door as I approached.

There was still enough daylight left for her to recognize me, and she let out a squeal of pleasure and threw her arms around me and kissed me, as if she had seen me only a week or two before.

"Scott Waring," she cried, "what brings you here?"

She had aged. She was in her sixties now, her round face fallen into folds and valleys, her buxom body lean and bent, her hair white.

"First we'll unload the car. Then we can talk."

She shook her head hopelessly over the mountain of food we piled up on her kitchen table. "Scott, Scott, I am not starving."

"I didn't know what else to bring."

"You're a dear man. I would have had some bread, some cheese and a cup of coffee for my dinner, and eat it all alone. No. I shall cook up a royal feast, and we shall eat and drink beer and talk. You'll stay tonight? The house is empty. I have rooms to spare."

"Of course I'll stay."

"The house is sold," she explained. "I got a good price, and in three weeks, I leave Germany forever."

"Where will you go?"

"I thought of New York—but no. I can no longer live as a Jew in a Christian land. I've visited Israel." She shrugged. "The language is impossible, but I'll find a few old people who speak German."

I got my luggage and carried it into the house, into a room

that had been her son's room. With a rush of energy, she put clean linen on the bed.

"You'll be comfortable here. Upstairs, it gets hot, but here it stays cool. Take a bath. Change your clothes. Take your time. Meanwhile, I'll cook."

She bustled out of the room, leaving me to open a suitcase and find a clean shirt. It was a pleasant room, the walls of walnut-stained wood, a pair of skis leaning in one corner, as, I supposed, her son had left them. There was a large framed photo on the wall of a soccer team, teen-age boys in shorts and jerseys, and on a bureau, two photographs, one of Paul with a pretty girl, and the other of Berthe with Paul, he a youngster and she a beautiful woman.

Soaking in the tub, I thought about my peculiar relationship to this woman. She had saved my life; without questions or discussion, without any kind of temporizing or indecision, she had saved my life; and now, at this moment, soaking in an oversized tub of hot water, smelling—even through the closed door—the delicious scent of sauerkraut, ham and sausage, life was very good. But to me, the ease and goodness of simply being alive had always been clouded with the guilt of my being alive and Martha dead. It came to me as it always had at such moments, but clouded now and very far off, and, I think, without the guilt. I could say, rest in peace, and smile at the memory of that lovely, bright and delightful woman to whom I had been married for a little while.

Berthe Baum had put candles on the table, which was set

on an embroidered linen cloth, with blue Meissen ware, crystal goblets and real sterling dinnerware. A pot of ham, sausage, sauerkraut, dumplings and apples simmered on the stove, and on the table, a platter of pickled herring, onions and black bread. She filled the goblets from a champagne bottle.

"Better this than beer tonight. The dishes and the silver and the goblets are all sold with the house, but we use them this once. Scott Waring, you are my first guest in a long time." She raised her glass. "*L'chaim*—to life!"

I drank. "And to you, Berthe Baum," I added.

"You like herring?"

"I love it."

"Good. Good. The secret of survival is the future, not the past. We are old friends. I will give you my address in Israel, and someday you will visit me there."

I couldn't help laughing; she shook her head and spread her hands.

"You asked me whether I like herring. Then you invite me to Israel and you tell me the secret of survival."

She shrugged. "It all goes together. There is a mystique to herring. The great herring eaters are the English, the Dutch, the Danes, Norwegians, the Swedes and the Jews. Now don't look at me as if I am simply a crazy old lady. The Nazis have come and gone, and we sit here with fine old Meissen and real silver and good food. I was not always a whore monger."

"No, you are a remarkable woman. I never thought of you as a whore monger."

"The pot has a half hour more to cook, so I'll tell you a story, and we can both get a little drunk. My husband was the chief of the waterworks in Coburg. He was a good, decent man—oh, not a romantic lover or anything of that sort, but a good, solid, substantial man, a good, typical German *Hausherr,* except that he was Jewish. One night, the SS came for him and took him away. I never saw him again. Paul was hidden in the root cellar behind the house. I wanted to save Paul and I wanted to save myself. So instead of waiting for them to come and take us, as they would have, I went to see the chief of the SS in Coburg." She was smiling now.

"And the countries that eat herring?" I asked her.

"Ah? I confuse you, don't I? The whole existence of the Jew is something of a non sequitur. But those six countries who comprise my little joke about the herring—" She took the platter and helped me to more herring. "I pickle it myself," she said. "Those countries are merchant countries. They understand the nature of contracts, and that's how they survive without great land and great populations. Has it anything to do with herring? God only knows. But consider, my dear Scott, that when Antonio made his contract with Shylock, no one forced him, no one threatened him. He was stupid enough to wager a pound of flesh." Her eyes brimmed with tears. She shook her head with annoyance and wiped the tears away.

"You don't have to tell me—"

"Oh, stop it, Scott Waring. No one is clever enough, and in the end the animals win. But I'll tell you what I did. I went to see Colonel Franz Schturm, the local SS commander, and I made a deal with him. I said that if he let me alone and left Paul alone, I'd turn my house into a brothel and take him as a partner and guarantee him two thousand marks a week and all the free screwing he desired."

"And he agreed?"

"Of course, he agreed. If I were not Jewish, his price would have been twenty marks a week."

"Two thousand marks a week?"

She shook her head and smiled. "We never earned two thousand marks a week, but for the first time in his life, Colonel Schturm owned a whorehouse. He spent almost every evening here, and beat his wife if she dared question why he almost never spent a leave at home." She rose and went to the stove. When she lifted the lid of the pot, the heady aroma filled the room. "Almost ready," she told me. A few minutes later, she filled my plate with dumpling, pork, sausage, potato, carrots and onion—and whatever else she used for the magic flavor.

So I sat at her table, stuffing myself with heavy, delicious food and getting drunk. We put aside the champagne for the meat and dumplings and switched to the beer I had brought. I thought of describing the scene to my mother, her son sitting with this wise old madam, talking German, eating German cooking, drinking beer. No way, ever. The ghost of Max Lieberman hovered over me. That was something else.

"And in the end," she said, "they took Paul."

"How did that happen?"

"The good Colonel Schturm was covering himself. He turned him in. You believe that you understand a swine, you say, he is my swine, but a swine is nobody's swine."

"Or else, simply a swine," I agreed. "You see, nobody tells us what they did to Shylock, or his wife, or his father, or his mother, but simply that he is a cruel bastard who wants his pound of flesh. I never thought of it that way. But when I think of Buchenwald and Dachau—"

"Would you take your pound of flesh, Scott?" We were both drunk at this point, comfortably drunk, full of food, full of that fine old German word, *Gemütlichkeit,* at least toward each other.

"You want me to be Jewish?"

"I don't think so," she said. "You're a fine, young, innocent American gentleman. Why should I want you to be any other way? I have a Sacher torte, imported from Vienna."

"And you want me to eat it—after all this?"

"A small piece. It's the only thing Viennese that I admire. A small piece?"

"Well, perhaps, a very small piece."

She brought out the cake and cut it. "Coffee?" she asked.

"Absolutely."

"And you want to be Jewish?" she asked as she handed me the cake.

"I'm not sure."

"In Munich, in the Alte Pinakothek, there is a painting of an old Jew with a crown of thorns—"

She never stopped surprising me. "I know the painting," I told her.

"Oh? Then we have a thought together. Do you suppose they killed him because he was Jewish?"

"So the Bible says."

"Or because he wanted a pound of flesh?"

"Now, you lost me," I said. "This chocolate cake is absolutely wonderful."

"Another piece?"

"If you twist my arm."

She smiled. "That's charming. That's an Americanism, isn't it?"

"I guess—yes."

"Do you believe in God, Herr Waring?"

"Now that is one for the books."

"Another Americanism?"

"I guess a sort of idiom. They never sound quite right in German. You know, dear lady, I think when two people have shared something and they drink and eat and feel good, they always end up with God. You and I are from the opposite ends of the earth. You are Jewish and I am Christian. You owe me nothing. I owe you a human life, mine. In the scale of things, in the world we live in today, a human life is not worth a great deal—unless it happens to be one's own. And now you ask me whether I believe in God?"

"You keep repeating the question. That's very Jewish."

"I am drunk and befuddled, and I don't think that in all

my life I ever asked myself seriously, do I believe in God? How can I answer that question? I spent an hour this morning in Dachau. As a small boy, I was sent to one of the best private schools in New York City. I was coddled and loved and told how bright I was. I was sheltered and protected, and every morning I took a warm shower. When I crawled into my bed at night, I said, Now I lay me down to sleep, I pray the Lord my soul to keep. Should I die before I wake, I pray the Lord my soul to take. That had absolutely nothing to do with God. It had to do with my mother, who sat by my bed while I said it. She was a tall, beautiful woman with blue eyes and blond hair. When I was nineteen years old, in Boston, where I was in college, I went to see a production of *The Merchant of Venice,* and at the time, I think—I say, I think, because I'm a little muddled, but I thought at the time that Shylock was a kind of disgusting old man, and what would it profit him to have his pound of flesh? Antonio was young and handsome. Shylock wanted his life. Portia spoke that wonderful speech about the quality of mercy—" I shook my head hopelessly. I had lost what I was trying to say.

"Yes," Berthe agreed. "It's a wonderful speech. *The Merchant of Venice* was very popular here in Germany. They played it everywhere. I went to see it with my husband. He was an important official, and he said we were not to think of ourselves as the kind of Jew Shylock was. We were educated, civilized Germans, and you would be surprised how eloquent Shakespeare is in German. Oh, enough. You're tired. Do you want to go to bed?"

"You were talking about Colonel Schturm before."

"Yes. I forgot what I was going to say."

"No, Berthe," I insisted, "no, you haven't forgotten."

She studied me in silence for a little while. The *Gemütlichkeit* was gone. "Think about Shylock, dear Scott. Colonel Schturm came to me. The American troops were in Coburg. He pleaded with me. He wept. He reminded me that he had kept me alive. He begged me to hide him, to be merciful."

"And you hid him?"

"Yes, I put him in the root cellar, where I had once hidden my only son, Paul."

"Yes. Go on, Berthe."

"The Americans came by and stopped at the house. They were in two of those cars you call jeeps—six of them, I believe. They were military police. They had a list of men, and they questioned me. Schturm's name was on the list. I took them to the root cellar, and I called out, Come out, Colonel Schturm. There are people here to see you. He came out and fell on his knees, pleading with the Americans not to kill him."

"They didn't kill him, did they?"

"No, Scott. They didn't kill him. They took him to Munich, where he was tried. He was found guilty and hanged." And then she added, "And what good did it do me? It did not bring Paul back. I was not very noble. I wanted revenge for the death of my son, but there is really no such thing. The dead are dead. My husband, Paul, your wife, Martha—they're all dead, and this morning you tore your heart open in Dachau, because you are kind and decent, and here we are drunk and eating good food and full of warm life. Leave the dead alone, Herr Waring. Right now is really all that means anything."

"You are a very wise woman," I said, "and I feel closer to you than I ever felt to anyone, except a young girl, whose name is Janet, and who was born in Munich. She was taken to the camp at Dachau when she was eleven years old, and she became the plaything of the commander of the camp, who raped her and kept her alive for his pleasure. Eventually, she came to America and learned to be a dancer. I fell in love with her. Someday, I will marry her."

Berthe began to cry. I took my handkerchief and reached over and wiped away her tears.

"The lives we have lived," she said.

"A few nights ago, I took all the pictures I have of Martha, and I looked at them and I learned about love. For years after the war, I lived in a kind of depression. Then I went to a psychiatrist, a man called Dr. Lieberman, a Jew, who tried to untangle all the knots that were tied up in my mind. What was I saying? I think I'm drunk. Am I boring you?"

She took my hand, lifted it and pressed it to her lips. Then she shook her head. "Please, go on, Scott."

"I was talking about the pictures of Martha. I looked at each picture. I was filled with sadness, but also with love. I was able to love this dead woman who had been my wife for a little while, and suddenly I was released. Do you understand what I am trying to say?"

"I think I do, Scott."

"I'm trying myself to understand what happened to me."

She nodded.

"You understand, don't you?"

"Yes."

"It isn't only that you saved my life. You gave me the gift of love. You asked me whether I believed in God, and I gave you some kind of foolish answer. Do you believe in God, Berthe?"

"Dear boy, I think we have talked enough. You have made me very happy today, and a few hours of happiness are very precious for this old lady. If I believed in God, how could I forgive him for what he has done? There was a day, Scott, when loneliness became too much for me. It was a Sunday, and Sundays are the worst. I walked into Coburg, and I saw people going into a church. I went with them into the church. I had never done that before. I wanted to see how Germans spoke to their God after the Holocaust, and I sat very quietly, listening to the singing and to the prayers—oh, enough. I'm tired now. Go to bed, Scott Waring."

# IV

t six o'clock in the morning, when I came out of my room, Berthe Baum was already awake and up, the kitchen full of the smell of coffee and fried sausage, the table set for my breakfast. She looked younger than the night before; she had put on makeup. There is a quality that a beautiful woman never loses, a certain sense of herself as more than memory. My mother had that quality; Berthe had that quality. She smiled at me with warm possessiveness, and poured coffee and set out a plate of sausage and eggs and a basket of tiny brown rolls, making of the food a greeting for the morning. She was a woman to whom food was more than nourishment; it was a symbol and a statement of life and the immediacy of life, and I recalled that Janet Goldman shared that attitude toward food. Perhaps long, long ago, my own ancestors had looked upon food in the same way.

"When is your plane?" she asked me.

"Seven o'clock. With the time difference, I'll be in New

York a few hours later. It seems impossible, when I think of the long ocean trips, eleven days on the troop carrier to North Africa."

"And what do you have in New York, Herr Waring?"

"I think—" I had a mouthful of food. "I think a woman who loves me."

She nodded. "That's a good thing to have waiting for you. But believe me, if I were thirty years younger—ah, well, as God wills it."

"The God you don't believe in?"

"Did I ever say that? I don't think a Jew can be an atheist. We get very angry at this strange and whimsical God of ours, and we distrust him and curse him, but after all, we invented him. Maybe that's why they hate us." She smiled then, and added, "Do you know, Scott, you are really the only man I ever opened my heart to. Not my husband, not any other man. Last night, trying to sleep, I made myself a fantasy that you had come all the way back to Germany to see me again. But that's not so, and don't tell me it is, because I'll know it's a lie."

"Partly. That's not a lie. Won't you eat anything?" I asked her.

"Coffee is my breakfast."

"Partly—partly to stop here again. I didn't know whether you were alive or dead. I had decided that if you were alive and needed money—well, I have a traveler's check in my wallet for five thousand dollars. My father left me a small inheritance, so I won't miss the money."

She shook her head. "I don't need money, Scott. But after

you leave, I'll cry my heart out. If we were to talk all day and all night, I could not tell you what you have done for me."

"Or what you have done for me."

"Thank you."

"And the other part of my coming here—well, as much as I can explain, it was to go to Dachau and to walk through that cursed place with the ghost of a little girl of eleven years who was raped by an SS man."

She stared at me for a few moments, silent, her face full of pain.

They tell me that June is the best month in Germany, and certainly I was blessed with cool, splendid weather when I left Berthe Baum and drove across Germany, through Bavaria and Hesse to Frankfurt. Berthe embraced me before I left. She had prepared a picnic basket of food, a bottle of wine, two bottles of beer, cold meat and cheese and black bread and fruit and cookies and a slice of the impossible Viennese chocolate cake, enough food to feed a family of four.

Frankfurt is no great distance from Coburg, but the road winds and twists through some of the prettiest country in Germany, rolling hills and rich farmland. I drove slowly, taking the time to think and trying to understand, at long last, who Scott Waring was, and what he intended. I stopped at a little park enclave near Würzburg to have a picnic lunch, and there was a young couple with a child of three years or so, and I gave them what was left of my basket, for which they were most grateful. They couldn't thank me enough. They spoke of what a hard time they were having, and it struck me as curious that I had no animosity for them. Frankfurt, which I had last seen eight years ago as a ruined city, was rebuilt to an extent that hid almost all traces of war. I drove on through to the Rhine-Main Airport, where I turned in my car, thinking all the while of the amazing energy of this strange people. The plane took off on time, and I slept comfortably through most of the trip to Idlewild Airport in Queens.

It was almost midnight when I turned the key in my apartment, and as I opened the door, the telephone was ringing. I dropped my bags and ran to answer it, but too late. I thought about it for a minute or so, and then I called Janet. "Were you trying to reach me?" I asked her.

"Scott! Yes, only a moment ago. I've been calling you all week. Where have you been? Are you all right?"

"Oh, I'm fine," I said. "How are you?"

"Never mind me. Of course, I'm all right. But where have you been? They said at your office you had taken a vacation. But without telling me, without a word to me."

"I had to be alone. But I'm back now. I'm all right."

"Thank God."

"Is it too late? Can I come over?"

"Now?"

"Now, yes."

"Sure. Yes, come now."

It was very strange indeed. In Coburg the sun would be

rising, but I wasn't tired. I left my bags where I had dropped them and walked the few blocks to Minetta Lane, and Janet Goldman opened the door for me, and stood in the doorway looking at me, and then reached out and touched my face. Then I took her in my arms and held her and kissed her.

"Where were you?" she whispered. "I thought— oh, God, I don't know what I thought! I was so frightened." She drew back and studied me. "Your face is healed. Oh, I'm so glad to see you." She was in a robe, her face scrubbed clean and shining, her eyes wet. "Dear Scott," she said.

"You don't hate me?"

"Hate you?"

"That was a stupid question, wasn't it."

"Yes, stupid."

"Well, I'm not the brightest man on earth, but I try."

"Yes."

"I want to ask you something."

"Yes."

"Will you marry me?"

"What?"

"Will you marry me. Just that. Will you?"

"Yes. You know I will. Why should I want anything else in the world?"

"Tomorrow?"

"Yes, tomorrow, if you want to."

"Thank God." I reached out to embrace her, but she pulled away.

"Aren't you hungry? Thirsty? Do you want a drink?"

"Oh, no. No," I said. "I just want to be sure."

"Of what?"

"That you'll marry me."

"I'm sure, Scott. I'm very sure." She took my hands in hers. "Don't you believe me? I never lied to you."

"I believe you."

"Then come to bed with me."

I took off my clothes and crawled into her bed, and lay there with Janet in my arms. I was with her, and I was free.